HOW OLD
IS THIS
HOUSE?

HOW OLD IS THIS HOUSE?

HUGH HOWARD

for Home Renovation Associates

The Noonday Press
Farrar, Straus and Giroux
New York

Library of Congress Cataloging-in-Publication Data
Howard, Hugh.
How old is this house? : a skeleton key to dating, identifying,
and understanding three centuries of the American house / by Hugh
Howard for Home Renovation Associates.—1st ed.
p. cm.
Bibliography: p.
Includes index.
1. Architecture, Domestic—United States—Dating.
2. Architecture, Domestic—United States—Expertising.   I. Home
Renovation Associates.   II. Title.
NA7205.H73   1989
728'.028—dc19   88-7865
ISBN: 0-374-52179-4 (Paperback)
ISBN: 0-374-17324-9 (Hardcover)

*This book is for
Ann D. Howard, who
taught me to look at—
and to care about—
old houses*

Acknowledgments

Two men, in particular, have shared with me much of their hard-earned knowledge of old houses: Donald Carpentier, the Squire of Eastfield Village in East Nassau, New York, and William McMillen, Supervisor of Restoration at Richmondtown on Staten Island, New York. Without them, this book could not have been written.

Many others have also helped me learn to look at and understand things old and American, buildings and otherwise. Among them are Robert Adam, Phyllis Azarian, John Curtis, Frank and Harriet Grant, Jerry Grant, Robert Herron, Martha Lawrence, Donald MacCready, Henry Mercer, and John Mesick. To all of these generous and insightful people, my thanks.

My appreciation, too, to Roger W. Straus, III, for helping pilot this particular book in a direction that, at first, no one—including me—knew it was to travel. I am indebted as well to Elisabeth Dyssegaard, who edited the manuscript with a careful eye and genuine concern for getting it just right. Finally, my especial thanks to Marge Anderson, who brought her usual impeccable good taste to the design of this book.

CONTENTS

It has always seemed to me that in studying architecture we should learn to read buildings themselves, rather than mere words about them.

—Hugh Morrison, from
Early American Architecture

INTRODUCTION

This is a book for people who have learned (or are learning) that there is something special about older houses. The appeal may be emotional or aesthetic. You may be able to describe quite precisely what the attraction is, or it may be beyond words. But we house fanciers know who we are.

How Old Is This House? is intended for the person who wants to understand where his or her house fits into the time line of architectural history. From the grandest of eighteenth-century colonials to the practical bungalows of the 1920s, there has been an evolution in the American house, one that has had evident moments of transition that separate the eras. Helping you fit your and your neighbors' houses into that time continuum is one goal of this book. Another is to help distinguish the old from the not-so-old within individual houses.

One value of dating a house is to enable a preservation, restoration, or renovation program to use the logic of history to advantage. Renovations that are respectful of a house's history tend to increase its value, while those that flout the past may well do the opposite. A sensitivity to the history of a place can also provide less tangible rewards. It may cost you more to do it "right" in an historic sense, but the dividends are many and varied.

We will talk in the closing chapter about putting historical knowledge of a house to use—but first we must gather it. We can investigate on three fronts, pursuing issues of style, documentary evidence, and physical evidence.

The Prologue that follows introduces a few houses and homeowners, along with some key issues that most of us encounter as we explore and come to understand our aged houses. Chapter 1 offers a preliminary look at the process of dating. It requires that one develop a variety of instincts, one borrowed from the scientist, one from the craftsman, and yet another from the historian. From there, we move to the heart of the matter.

There are other sources that can help you appreciate the age and qualities of your home, but it is the house itself whence the best observations are to be made. To that end, Chapter 2 begins the hands-on approach, an inspection of the artifact.

By looking closely at your house, at its details, a specifically chronological understanding can emerge of the house and its changes over the years. Chapter 2 begins outside, advising how and where to look in investigating your house. Whether it's a little archaeological dig in the yard or just a general inspection of the siding and exterior shape, much can be learned about a house—even when you think you already know every detail.

Chapters 3, 4, and 5 are intended to provide you with a basic, chronological knowledge of the American house as it has evolved over the centuries. To understand a house built in 1920, not to mention one built in 1720, it is valuable to have traveled through time and to have seen what was there, what wasn't, and when. That is one principal goal of these chapters; another is to help you identify the style of your house.

Just as narrow ties and wide lapels and button shoes tell us something about a man's wardrobe, so do the shapes and decorations on a house. If your house is clearly identifiable as, say, American Gothic, then it probably was built between 1840 and 1860. In a series of separate sections, under the heading "Style Notes," the major American architectural styles are described and the key identifying characteristics specified for easy house identification.

As you learn to distinguish styles, it is equally important that you register the individual pieces of physical evidence that come before your eyes; they, too, are critical to establishing the age of a house and its parts. Throughout these chapters are asides on such issues as hardware, fireplaces, moldings, and other details that can be surprisingly revealing about the history of a house.

The pursuit of documentary evidence may be the easiest to learn but also the most time consuming part of the dating process. In Chapter 6, you will learn how dusty deeds at the county archive can produce substantial information about the age of your house and those who lived there, and may reinforce your later discoveries. Chapter 7 offers some suggestions for one further, rather informal avenue of research, namely, oral history. Drawing upon the recollections of previous residents and neighbors and townspeople often produces surprising revelations about a house and its earlier times.

Armed with their words and public records, you're ready to put your house into an architectural perspective. Chapter 8 is a summing up and offers a consideration of what your house's age means in terms of today and tomorrow. At the close of the book, there is a glossary of architectural and building terms; bibliographic materials, should you wish to pursue further research; and a number of organizations for further help, should you require it. Taken together, these sources might well tell you a good deal you didn't know about your home.

But now it's time to go a-hunting, for houses in general and for knowledge of yours. Just how old is it, anyway?

PROLOGUE

Determining the vintage of a house is more than a matter of chronology. Establishing the year in which it was constructed is just a starting point (and not the only one) in understanding and appreciating a house. It's like getting to know a person of a certain age: that he or she was born in a given year is a useful piece of information—but a birth date of, say, 1920 is worth less to us than its implications about the life experience of having lived through the Depression and World War II.

Every house has its own peculiar circumstances. No two are created equal, and no house experiences the same ebb and flow of owners and residents. It isn't only the whims of humanity that affect the life of a house over the years. Mother Nature, too, assaults and ages any structure.

Apprehending the character, quality, and vintage of a house requires an alert intelligence, a capacity for observing the obvious, and a willingness to invest time and energy in the search. Key discoveries may be made talking to a nosy neighbor or by the family dog burying a bone in the garden. Guidance may come from a wide range of sources, as the following true tales of discovery suggest.

Elaine and Paul Andersen live in suburban Des Plaines, just outside of Chicago. When they bought their first home several years ago, they knew it was about fifty years old and that it was a bungalow. They also knew that it was the only house they had seen that they could afford, so they bought it.

Once they moved in, they began to consider renovating. There was only one bathroom, and the upstairs had never been properly finished. Instinctively, they also wanted to put their own stamp on the place. Twenty years ago this would probably have led a good middle-class husband like Paul to hustle down to the local building supply outlet, and the remodeling would have commenced without further ado.

Today, however, there's a new step in the process of renovating an older home. You see, along with the epithets "mutual fund" and "random access memory," "architectural integrity" has become a word for the hoi polloi. Most people these days consider the "fabric" and the "style" of a place before they renovate (for a glossary of these and other terms, see page 185), and Paul and Elaine were no exception. Today people pay a certain homage to the builder's intentions, considering not only their own desires but what is *appropriate* to a particular house of a particular era.

The Andersens decided to do a bit of research into bungalows. They weren't looking to restore their place to its original state, nor were they considering a slavish imitation of some other house of the period. On the other hand, as Elaine puts it, "When you travel to Paris, you sort of owe them the courtesy of at least speaking a few words of the language, don't you?"

Elaine and Paul got lucky. While cleaning out one of the storage areas in the eaves, they found an old receipt tacked to a rafter. It was for the purchase of the house. It confused them because its date, 1922, was the same as the year of construction, and the seller was Sears, Roebuck and Company. But Elaine did some research and discovered the explanation.

For the first four decades of this century, Sears made "kit houses," buildings sold as precut but unassembled materials, ready to put together, not unlike the molded plastic car models sold for twelve-year-old hobbyists. Elaine hypothesized that theirs had been a Sears kit house. Then Paul came across a recent book published by the Preservation Press, the publications arm of the National Trust for Historic Preservation.

Called *Houses by Mail,* it pictured and described dozens of Sears mail-order houses. Elaine soon found their exact house in it, the model called "The Uriel," which sold for $1,473 when new.

In a second-hand bookstore, Elaine came across some sales catalogues and pamphlets about Honor-Bilt Homes, one of the trade names under which Sears sold houses. For less than twenty-five dollars, Elaine and Paul had a detailed, illustrated look at what their house would have been like when new.

With these primary sources on hand, their renovation was informed by more than instinct. They compared their ideas to the original plans. They used them to help select suitable lighting fixtures. The new ones weren't identical to those in the catalogue, but there was a resemblance. The new window in the dining room used the shape and location found in another, fancier Honor-Bilt home. For the deck off the back of the house, they borrowed a railing style from the book and a roofline for the screened portion that made it all very much of a piece.

There it is, "The Uriel," a house named after an archangel.
It was sold as a kit by Sears in its line of Honor-Bilt Homes
in the early 1920s. The price range was $1,374 to $1,527;
finish on the second floor was optional. *Credit: Sears, Roebuck.*

Paul and Elaine's discovery wasn't precisely a matter of age. They had known how old their house was before they bought it. Their findings were more subtle, more matters of detail and shading than of chronology. As the ever articulate Elaine Andersen told me, "It's like anything else. You do better when you know *something*—even a little—about the business at hand."

I've been aware of the house for years. It's located only a few doors from the train station, and each time I come or go on the Amtrak line, I feel a twinge of admiration for the solid, three-story brick house and its ongoing restoration.

The full portico at its entry has Ionic columns, and its doorway has both sidelights and a rectangular transom. The first- and second-floor windows are six-over-sixes—that is 6/6s (there are six panes of glass in both the upper and lower sashes of each double-hung window unit). "Eyebrow" windows peer out from the frieze of the third floor. As we'll see in our style discussions in Chapter 4, the house is a fine example of Greek Revival.

When I got to know its owner, a restoration contractor named Jeremiah Rusconi, I learned more about the house. It was built by a successful merchant who set his impressive home near the Hudson River. The façade looks west over a broad bend in the river that brought him and his town, Hudson, New York, their wealth in the early nineteenth century.

How old is the house? Given its location midway between Albany and New York City, it is reasonable to assume that the owner of the house and its builders were aware of the major cultural and architectural trends of the early nineteenth century. That suggests the house could have been built in the early years of the Greek Revival era, which ran from roughly 1830 to 1860. (In contrast, such a house built further west, for example, in Ohio or Michigan, would have been built late in the era.)

Identifying the style of the house as Greek Revival was useful in assigning an approximate date, but it was physical

This elegant, brick townhouse is located in Hudson, New York, on the banks of the Hudson River. Built in 1835, its graceful lines, Ionic portico, and third-story "eyebrow" windows proclaim its Greek Revival style to all who pass.

evidence that provided the exact date. Rusconi discovered the key clue in his attic. The boards that line the underside of the roof were smoothed by what was then a new device, the machine thickness planer (see page 95). As if to bear witness to the new technology, the boards, to this day, bear the stenciled name, date, and location of the mill that produced them. The city was Albany, New York, and the date, 1835.

When they discovered she could no longer take care of herself, Grandma St. John's family arranged for her to live with relatives. (With her usual good humor, she called herself "The Traveling Grandma," as she moved periodically from the house of one of her children to that of another.) Her empty house was then offered to the only married family member who didn't own a home, her great-grandchild Sharon. Sharon Niemi immediately bought the place, happy for the opportunity not only to own a house of her own but one full of family memories.

In talking to her great-grandmother and other family members, she learned that her great-grandparents had bought the little house in Westminster, Massachusetts, in 1912. When Sharon acquired the house some seven decades later, the cypress doors, the kitchen cabinets, the plaster walls, and the hardwood floors that had been in place in 1912 were still there. A cast-iron cookstove dominated the kitchen. The place was, despite several layers of more recent wallpaper, an essay on home design in pre-World War I America.

Sharon's needs were different than her grandmother's, and times had changed. Energy costs were different, too, so she replaced the windows and insulated the house. In doing this, she discovered that there was more than family history to the little house.

When it came time to remove the cracked and sagging plaster ceiling, she made her happiest discovery. The plaster had been supported by wooden strips called "lath" (see page 102 for a discussion of plaster and lath). Running perpendicular to the lath were "sleepers," plain pine boards that provided a level, regular surface to which the lath was nailed. The sleepers, in turn, had been nailed to a totally different sort of wooden framework.

The actual frame, Sharon discovered, was made of large-dimension timbers. Rather than the 2-inch-thick, standardized lumber that houses are usually built of today, the structure consisted of timbers that had been shaped with axes, some of which were almost 12 inches square. Some even retained the rounded shape of tree trunks. The timbers were connected not by nails but by whittled oak pins and "mortise-and-tenon" joints, in which the wood is shaped so that the end of one timber forms a tonguelike tenon that fits into an opening, the mortise, cut into the other.

The discovery of the timber frame was a wonderful revelation to Sharon, who immediately decided the deep reddish hues of the old wood weren't going to be obscured by a new layer of gypsum board. She learned that her find meant that the house was probably built much earlier than 1912. (Timber frames, which are also known as post-and-beam frames, were *the* material employed to frame wooden houses in this country until late in the nineteenth century, when they ceased to be used.) So she set about unearthing what she could about her house's earlier life.

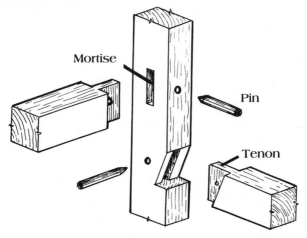

Mortise-and-tenon joints were used to hold together all the major timbers in the early American "timber-frame" house. Until about 1800, nails were all handmade (and therefore very expensive), so the extremely strong, pinned wooden joint was both economical and practical, well suited to the large wooden members of the timber-frame.

Written records of the house prior to 1912 were scant, but she learned that the timber-framed portion had a wing added in 1911. The old part of the house had been a small building of minor significance; the tax records at the town hall and the files at the local historical society made little mention of it. However, since the house had been in the family for most of the century, Sharon didn't meet with a dead end.

What archival paperwork couldn't tell her, her family could. She acquired bits of architectural history, leavened with recollections of cookies and Christmas trees. When her great-grandparents bought the place, it had just been moved from another location near the village center. The house had been moved to its present location in 1911, and during the next year was remodeled into the comfortable house the St. Johns purchased.

But the story hadn't begun in the village; that was actually the *third* location of the building. It had been a tackle-and-bait shop near a reservoir, having been moved there from its original location as a kitchen ell on a gracious 1810 house several miles away. While little of the story could be proved beyond the shadow of a doubt, the pieces fit together with few apparent inconsistencies.

The house itself offered more clues. In addition to the rough timber frame, the evidence included up-and-down saw marks on the sleepers that had lined the walls beneath the old plaster (see discussion of saw marks, page 10), and these boards had been fastened to the beams with old-fashioned cut nails (see discussion of nail types, page 54). All the evidence suggested that the building was constructed during the first quarter of the nineteenth century.

If you have any doubt in your mind as to why the age of a house is important, you're probably reading the wrong book. But before you give up on this one, consider the following situation.

About one hundred miles directly north of New York City is the country town of Claverack, New York. Settled in the late eighteenth century, the town still boasts a handsome array of Colonial and early American houses. Many are in the Dutch style (not surprising, given the name of the town and the number of Dutch structures in the Hudson Valley). Others are Georgian (the style prevalent from about 1725 to 1780) and Adamesque (1780–1820).

One morning in 1987, plaster and other detritus began thundering to the ground from an upstairs window of one of these early houses. Neighbors soon learned that the house was being dismantled and was to be moved to an open field in a nearby town. Some of them were outraged, and the controversy that shortly ensued galvanized a number of members of the community.

A local realtor, Peggy Lampman, explained to me her and other townspeople's concern. "The house has been there since the 1770s, and it's in very good condition. But the controversy isn't only about the house but about the community. Moving a major house in a community like Claverack—it's like moving a house on [Boston's] Beacon Hill. That house is in a collection of great eighteenth-century houses. Moving it away is just an outrage."

The owner, Barry Sirmon, sees it differently. "Location was the primary problem," he says. When he decided he wanted to put the original porch back on the house (it had been removed in an early twentieth-century "colonialization"), he discovered he couldn't do it. "The edge of the road is only eighteen feet away, the right of way ten feet closer." The only solution, as he saw it, was to move the house to another setting with ample room, away from the heavily traveled road on which it sat in Claverack.

Some townspeople moved to stop the dismantling. While there was a question as to whether Sirmon had a valid building permit (and whether he needed one for a dismantling), the house was not in an historic district and there were no restrictions on the books, as there are in some towns, that required municipal approval for the remodeling, restoration, or dismantling of historic structures. After a short delay, the dismantling resumed, and today the house sits isolated at the heart of a handsome piece of property eleven miles away, in Livingston, New York.

To me, it is a footnote to the story that is the most interesting part of it. The house had been known as the "John Day home," named after the man who lived in it around 1780.

It had been thought, on the basis of physical evidence, that he built the house, although no documents exist to prove he did. The paneling in the dining room quite evidently dated from about 1780, so that seemed to clinch it.

When the house was dismantled, however, it was discovered that beneath that "original" paneling were plaster and signs of earlier, cruder paneling. Beneath that earlier paneling were still other indications that the room had once been used to store grain. Apparently, that entire half of the house, as was common in Dutch houses ca. 1750, was a "granary." As if to confirm the hypothesis, the frame of the house revealed that at one time three barn doors had been located in that section, though they had long been obscured by more recent remodelings.

Sirmon and his advisors interpreted this and other evidence to mean that the place was built earlier, perhaps as early as 1750. If that was true, Sirmon surmised, then the house would have predated the rest of the houses on the street—and would, in fact, have been in a setting quite like the one to which the house has since been moved. Rather than being a violation of its architectural history, the move meant that history was being served. Or so goes the argument.

The opposing position remains sound, too. The community of fine houses evolved, together with Sirmon's house, for more than two centuries. Separating the house from that community is, in the eyes of many, a crime against architectural history.

These stories suggest something of the diversity of sources to be drawn upon in establishing how old a house is. There are deeds and other paperwork sources; there are matters of style; and there is physical evidence, whether it is pieces of paneling or newspapers plastered into the walls.

Yet the fact remains that there is no single, foolproof recipe for dating a house. If you elect to rely upon written records—wills, tax receipts, and the like—you may find that just when you get close, one ingredient will be lacking. Physical evidence and style will provide you with a range of years within which your house was built, but probably will offer conflicting evidence as well. And the chances are excellent there won't be a single answer, since many houses were built in stages over a period of a century or more.

The bottom line is that you must employ all the means available. At best, you will uncover an exact date; at worst, you will know a great deal more about your house than you did before. The point isn't a single date anyway. Rather, the goal of this book is to help you reach a better understanding of the character and quality of your house so that you can make the most informed decisions about its restoration or renovation.

1.

The
Disciplines
of Dating

There they were, alone in a densely forested land. It was, in the words of William Bradford in *Of Plymouth Plantation,* "a hidious and desolate wilderness, ful of wild beasts and willd men." Since there were no hotels in which to rest up from the long and uncomfortable sea voyage, the new arrivals worked with what they saw before them. In short order, some of those trees were sacrificed to build some uncomplicated wooden buildings.

That's a bit simplistic, of course, but as far as it goes, the scenario accurately describes what the Puritans were forced to do upon their arrival in the New World. Apparently they set a major precedent: most domestic construction in North America in the intervening three and a half centuries has involved turning trees into buildings.

Given that roughly 90 percent of all existing American houses are made of wood, we'll start with a scientific approach to that principal component. We'll go on to take both a practical and a historical look at the wooden house, and what it has to tell us about our houses today.

THE SCIENCE OF ARCHAEOMETRY

"Archaeometry" is a nascent science. It derives from the Greek words for measuring (or metering), as in "-metry," and for ancient or primitive, as in "archaeo-." It involves physics, chemistry, and geology. Art historians, restorers, archaeologists, and scientists collaborate to determine the identity, age, and method of production of materials, often in an effort to distinguish forgeries.

The archaeometric test we hear about most often is carbon-14 dating. Other high-tech tests include atomic absorption spectrophotometry, emission spectroscopy, x-ray diffraction, and microscopy. These tests have made the detection of forged ancient artifacts and old paintings close to foolproof.

While an archaeometric analysis of the Shroud of Turin may advance our knowledge of that legendary cloth, the same tests are of next to no value in dating an American house. In Europe there are truly ancient structures (for example, the stone buildings of ancient Greece and Rome or the wooden stave churches in Norway that date from the twelfth century). But on this side of the Atlantic, the buildings are either too young for much of this technology to be applicable or recent layers of paint and the innumerable other small and large changes made by generations of inhabitants render the test results confusing and useless. Not to mention that the costs for most of the tests and their technicians are usually prohibitively high for the average homeowner.

Yet there is a technological component to house restoration at its most sophisticated (and expensive) level. The technological vanguard of the preservation movement is well represented by the Society for the Preservation of New England Antiquities, which owns some eighty properties, two dozen of which are open to the public as museums.

In their restoration activities, the SPNEA's laboratories routinely examine chips of paint or whitewash. Their geologists identify the stonework. Archaeologists dig and infrared photos are taken of wall paintings. Any new piece of wood added to an old structure has a copper tag attached, with a date stamped onto it so the next investigator will have the clearest of clues to guide him or her in determining when that particular element was added.

One of the tests that SPNEA and others use is "dendrochronology" (a word derived from the Greek *dendro* for tree). It is an archaeometric test that can help date buildings. Employed in Britain and Germany for a number of years, it is relatively new in the United States, though the SPNEA and others now perform it, both for themselves and as a paid service for others.

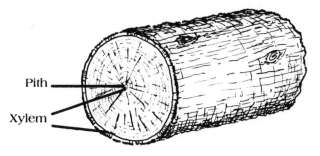

Pith

Xylem

The innermost part of the tree is the oldest. When harvested for building, it is the xylem that is cut into lumber.

In order to understand how dendrochronology works, a little tree sense is required. Looking at a stump or log in cross section, the center is the pith—a small, soft core of wood that disappears over time after the tree is cut down. It is the oldest part of the tree. The rings around it go from oldest to youngest, moving outward on the radius. Count the rings, and you know the age of the tree.

The growth of the tree takes place on the outer edge near the bark, with the bulk of the tree, the xylem, in between the pith and the bark. The xylem is the portion that is sawn into lumber and timber for building materials.

Dried and milled wood, and even wood that has spent centuries as the frame of a house, retains its telltale rings. A ring represents a growing season. On the pith side of each ring

3

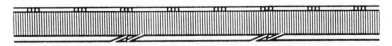

A NOTE
FOR
WORD FANCIERS

If mastering a verbal subtlety or two can brighten your day, here's a brief aside just for you. There is a hierarchy to wood after its visit to the sawmill. The largest sawmill products are called "timber"; the next are termed "lumber"; and the smallest are "boards." Technically, timber is wood of a dimension greater than 4 inches by 4 inches; boards are of a thickness of 1 inch or less; lumber falls in between.

Remember, however, that those are the dimensions before planing; the milled lumber one buys as building material today is planed to a smaller dimension. Thus, a two-by-four is actually 1 1/2 inches by 3 1/2 inches, having had 1/4 inch milled off each side (though it's still called lumber); one-inch boards are actually 3/4 of an inch thick. Most houses constructed with lumber that is 1 1/2 inches by 3 1/2 inches probably postdate World War II.

are the large, soft, and spongy cells of spring growth. They merge almost imperceptibly into the smaller and harder and darker cells of the summer and fall growth. The clearly defined lines between the rings indicate winter and the transition from the slower growth of fall to the spurt of the following spring.

It is the sequence of rings that the dendrochronologist "reads." Dendrochronologists speak of relatively good or bad growth years, since the width of the rings varies according to growing conditions. The variations for a particular series of years are the same for all trees of the same species grown in the same area.

In a recent study conducted in southern Maryland, sixty-four aged trees were felled. Their planting dates ranged back as far as 1717. The rings within each of the red and white oaks were measured with a dendrochronometer, and the measurements put directly into a computer. This provided the baseline data.

To date a structure, the dendrochronologist compares the ring patterns in the established baseline to the rings in the timber used in the frame of a building. When a correlation is found, the last year of tree growth indicates the time at which the timber was felled and used as a building material.

Dendrochronology isn't foolproof. As John Obed Curtis, the director of the Curatorial Department at Old Sturbridge Village, told me, "[Dendrochronology] turned out to be something of a disappointment. We tried it out on an eighteenth-century tavern building, and it didn't tell us anything we didn't already know from looking at it." (Of course it should be said that Curtis probably knew a great deal about that building long before the dendrochronologists appeared).

Another problem with dendrochronological findings can be that if the timber examined was originally used in a previous structure and reused in your house, the date will be for the first building, not yours. But in the Maryland study, dendrochronology identified several buildings as having been of quite different dates than had previously been believed. It also distinguished the dates of additions to certain structures, helping to explain broader issues such as the development of building techniques and even cultural processes.

A dendrochronologist may be worth consulting for very old houses. But, in general, dating and understanding a house is less a matter of science than of history.

THE SHAPING OF WOOD

Dozens of Amish men, some on foot and others riding in horse-drawn wagons, arrive on the farm. Dressed in baggy dark

5

trousers and suspenders, they wear wide-brimmed straw hats to protect them from the sun. Their attire is, by modern standards, goofy. Yet, one senses, these God-fearing men have a grace and style that renders costume irrelevant.

One of them, his beard long and his face wizened, calls back to his companion. "We have a barn to raise and a day to do it." It is a command; its message clear: "Let's get to work."

Moments later, thanks to the miracle of the cinematic jump cut, an enormous wall of timber is being raised by that Amish work force. They lift the preassembled wall of posts and beams to shoulder height, then insert poles to push it higher. Other men strain at ropes, helping to pull the timber-frame section, called a "bent," into place. Shortly another joins the first, and the two parallel bents are linked with other large timbers running perpendicular to the bents, the plates. We see Harrison Ford drilling a hole with a hand brace, then hammering home a wooden pin with a wooden mallet. He stops to share a glass of lemonade.

> In this ca. 1890 photograph, the building being raised is actually a barn. But only the scale makes this frame different from that in a typical house: the configuration of posts and beams and braces is the same, as is the hazardous and labor-intensive process of tilting the bents into place.

Though we see the day pass and night fall as the process concludes, the barn frame in the movie *Witness* goes up in minutes. Then the Amish load up their wagons and go home, a song on their lips.

The scene is affecting in part because of its role in the unfolding cross-cultural love affair between Harrison Ford, who plays a contemporary Philadelphia cop, and his Amish paramour-to-be, played by Kelly McGillis. But in many people the scene touches another elemental emotion having to do with house and home and doing it one's self.

The raising of the timber frame in the movie is accurate as far it goes. But no building was built in a day. Some are *raised* in a day; the work starts long before.

If Messrs. Black and Decker had their way, every handyman's toolbox would have a hand-held power saw (often called a Skilsaw). Today's workshop also has a table or a radial-arm saw, both of which are large, fixed pieces of equipment. All three of these power tools use circular blades, a configuration virtually unheard of in this country until about 1830.

The typical woodworker today also uses an electric jigsaw, saber saw, "saws-all," or all three. These reciprocating saws (they cut in an up-and-down, reciprocating motion) have straight-edged blades with teeth machined onto their front edges rather than onto the circumference of a circle. While reciprocating saws have been used for thousands of years, portable power saws are largely a twentieth-century phenomenon, as are electrically powered cutting tools.

We take them all for granted. Even before they learned of the range, portability, and disposability of today's tools, our ancestors would be amazed. The electricity that powers our tools is usually but an extension cord away, and that alone is a staggering change from only a century ago. Most of today's blades are made of steel, a material virtually unknown but a century and a quarter ago.

At the opposite end of the historical spectrum, the prehistoric carpenter's toolbox probably included a felling ax, broadax, handsaw, and hammer. By the sixteenth and seventeenth centuries, when the first settlers arrived in North America, the T-square and straightedge, the compass, plumb, chisel, gouge, and auger had been added to the toolbox. Today, a good-sized pickup truck would be required to carry the contents of a carpenter shop; then, a convenient carryall box and one strong arm was quite sufficient.

There were no lumberyards or building supply stores in Bradford's "hidious and desolate wilderness," so those simple tools had to be used. The trees were cut down and the bark and branches trimmed off with the felling ax. The trunks then had to be smoothed and squared by hand into recognizable timbers with the broadax. The resulting timbers were approximately rectangular in section, but the surface was distinctly rough-hewn.

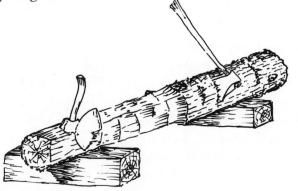

"Hewing the line," they called it. It was a laborious process that began with a line snapped onto the felled trunk with a chalk-covered string. Then a skilled carpenter made a series of cuts into the tree, swinging his felling ax (right) perpendicular to the length of the trunk. Next he hewed to the line, using his broadax (left), cutting parallel to its length. The result was a squared, hewn timber.

In addition, smaller wooden parts were necessary for flooring, wall coverings, and other purposes. For the earliest American houses, a long, two-man saw called the "pit saw" was indispensable for cutting the large timbers into lumber. Since it was necessary for one man to be beneath the log being cut, the pit saw required either a pit or a pair of tall trestles. The long saw was then worked vertically.

The pit saw required two workers. The "sawyer" was in charge and directed the cut of the saw from above. The laborer below did most of the work—and was showered with sawdust for his trouble.

Pit-sawing was a great deal of work, so it ceased in any locality as soon as power saws became available. There was a water-powered sawmill in Jamestown, Virginia, in 1625 that cut lumber. Others were constructed along the coast in the same era. Berwick, Maine, in 1650 saw the advent of a machine called a gang saw that featured several blades cutting several planks from a log at once. Pit-sawing disappeared in this country as water-powered reciprocating saws were constructed. By the late eighteenth or the early nineteenth century, when steam power came into general use, the pit saw was virtually extinct.

While the early sawmills all had straight, reciprocating blades that resembled the pit saw's, the circular saw came later. It was patented in England in 1777 and may have been used for some applications in the United States by the Shakers as early as 1795, but some sources suggest that it wasn't until 1814 that it made its appearance on these shores. In any case, it didn't come into general use until after 1830.

Initially, the circular saw was used for making drawer backs, shingles, plaster lath, and other items that required thinly cut pieces, but circular saw marks are found on many sorts of wood from the late 1830s. As early as 1860, circular

9

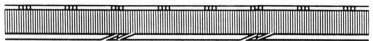

IDENTIFYING
SAW MARKS

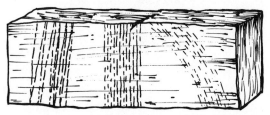

Pit-saw	Reciprocating	Circulating
Marks	Saw Marks	Saw Marks

The Pit Saw: Very early construction consists of hewn beams and pit-sawn boards, but while hand-hewing was practiced well into the third quarter of the nineteenth century, pit-sawn boards are rare after 1800. The pit saw was abandoned as soon as a local sawmill made machine-cut boards available.

If you think your house was built before 1800, try to identify pit-sawn boards. Likely locations are the back of paneling or sheathing (the inner lining of exterior walls), the undersides of floors in the house, the attic floor, or the sub-roof. A pit saw leaves angled saw marks. The cut lines should be as

saws were probably dominant, even at smaller mills. Since the late nineteenth century virtually all lumber has been cut with a circular saw, although most post-World War II lumber is planed smooth so that the marks are obliterated.

Life might have been simpler in early America, but given the work of hewing and pit-sawing house parts, it certainly wasn't easier.

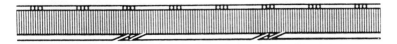

much as half an inch apart (sometimes more), but the width of the cuts will vary considerably. Era: Up to 1800, with regional variations.

Up-and-Down Saw: A reciprocating or up-and-down saw, like a pit saw, cuts at a very slight angle as the saw is tipped slightly forward. A typical reciprocating saw cuts at a rate of about sixty strokes a minute, with each stroke cutting about 1/8 inch. A handful of up-and-down sawmills still function; but the majority became extinct during the nineteenth century with the advent of the more efficient circular saw. Era: Common up to 1900.

Circular Saw: In the case of both pit-sawn and up-and-down-sawn boards, the cut lines are straight, while circular-sawn boards bear curved saw cuts. The date at which circular saws came into use in a given locale varies, but the frequent appearance of circular-saw marks in a structure suggest a date of 1840 or after. If you find a variety of saw marks, you might do well to check with your local historical society. Many studies have been made of early sawmills and their equipment as an aid in dating local buildings. Era: After ca. 1830.

THE EVOLUTION OF ARCHITECTURE

Architecture was probably first observed in nature, then imitated by a caveman. He positioned one stone over a gap between two others, and all at once he had mastered the first rudimentary principle any builder to this day must learn.

Buildings that result from the repeated use of that basic opening are called post-and-lintel structures. The upright stones, or, later, the wood or iron members, are the posts, while the lintel is the horizontal beam. Architectural historians seem to relish calling post-and-lintel structures "trabeated" (from the Latin *trabes,* for beam). Until late Greek or early Roman times, every structure with a roof was trabeated, built with either stone or wood (such structures made of timbers are called "post-and-beam").

For the most part, the Greeks and Egyptians were satisfied with post-and-lintel construction and the strongly rectilinear buildings it produced. The Romans developed a notable fondness for the arch (a curved rather than flat-topped opening); Medieval architecture saw the development of pointed arches; and during the Renaissance other structural advances were made. But it is the more primitive wooden trabeated framework that characterizes virtually all domestic American construction.

The hand-hewn early American wooden building has enormous timbers; the lowest member that sits atop the ground or foundation, the sill, is typically 7 inches by 10 inches or larger. The beams, posts, and rafters (the angled roof supports) generally decrease in size from there.

The evolution in this country of a framing system that called for relatively few large members is hardly surprising given the work involved in shaping the wood. It required an hour or two to shape an oak tree trunk into a beam; a tiny house required dozens of beams, a large one hundreds, so before the construction could get under way many days of labor had to be invested in shaping the building materials.

The labor-intensive hewing was a key aspect of constructing houses right up until the middle of the nineteenth century. At that time, technological advances in saws and the manufacture of nails made it possible to use many more, but much smaller, pieces of lumber instead of timbers. "Stick framing" is the term used for this later variety of framing, since it uses smaller dimension lumber rather than the timbers of "timber framing." Today, most houses are stick framed.

The timbers in Colonial America were usually cut locally, perhaps by the homesteader himself on his own property. They would be cut and shaped while green, since broadaxing a dried oak beam was a great deal more work than shaping one still soft with a high percentage of moisture. The hewn timber would then be dragged to the building site. The timbers for a house would have been shaped over a period of months. The first timber might be cut in August and broadaxed right away into a rectangular shape. The builder would then work through the winter when he could, and by April might have finished shaping the timbers.

Unless the owner had joinery training, a professional would probably have been hired to cut the mortise-and-tenon joints into the timbers. A mortise-and-tenon joint was the fastener of choice in a timber frame. It is the strongest and most pervasive wood joint and also can lay a claim to being one of the earliest of all joints. The stones at Stonehenge, which date from 3000 B.C., are held together by mortises and tenons.

Mortise-and-tenon joinery was labor intensive and involved using a saw and mallet and chisels to shape the mortises and tenons. A hole drilled through the joint then had a wooden pin hammered through it to secure the connection. The wooden pins were called "tree nails," which was shortened to "trenails" or "trunnels." These joints were so critical to the construction process that builders were often called joiners rather than carpenters. Today, the term "joiner" is usually reserved for the worker who makes doors and windows, which are among the few house parts that still require traditional joinery.

The joiner who made the frame would cut and fit the parts of each bent together, following a carefully laid-out plan. The foundation stones would be put in place and leveled, and the sills set on the foundation. All this was done in advance of the actual "raising" of the building, a chore that required a good deal of manpower, Amish or otherwise. When friends and neighbors arrived, they completed the assembly of the prefabricated parts and raised the bents into place.

Although settlers of diverse origins brought different

THE TIMBER FRAME
VERSUS
THE STICK-BUILT FRAME

Is it a timber or stick-built frame? One place to begin your investigation of a house's frame is in the attic. Are the rafters made of dimension lumber (two-by-fours, two-by-sixes, etc.)? If so, the roof is either new or of stick-built construction. If the frame is made of six-by-six or larger timbers connected by mortise-and-tenon joints and wooden pins, it's a timber frame. Perhaps the simplest way to distinguish a stick-built frame house from a timber-frame structure is by the thickness of its walls: those of the former are roughly 5 inches thick, while those of the latter are a minimum of 7 inches thick.

Timber Frame   Balloon Frame   Platform Frame

The Timber Frame: Try to get access to the posts or beams of the main structure. The best opportunity to do this is during demolition, but don't tear down a wall or ceiling just to examine the frame of the building. If you are able to examine closely the large timbers of the frame, check whether the surfaces are sawn flat, or is it evident that they were hewn?

The Balloon Frame: Although it was invented in Chicago in the 1830s, the balloon frame didn't come into common use in the West until roughly the Civil War era. It was ten or more years later that the "new" style made substantial inroads on the East Coast. The stick-built frame is distinguishable from the timber frame by the absence of timbers: the entire structure consists of smaller, sticklike members that are generally no thicker than 2 or 2 1/2 inches. Era: 1840s and after in the Midwest; 1860s and after in the West; 1870s and after in the East.

The Platform Frame: A second variety of stick-built framing, the platform frame, began to be used after the turn of the twentieth century. Also known as Western wood framing, platform framing rapidly became widely practiced. As in balloon framing, the wood used was dimension lumber, with pieces cut to 2-inch widths, with studs positioned on the sills at 16-inch intervals. But each story was built separately, with the wooden members supporting the second floor resting on top of the completed first floor wall. Then the second-story walls

were constructed on top of that floor. (In balloon framing, the vertical members extended all the way to the plate at the top of the uppermost story wall, rather than terminating at each floor level.) Unless one has access to the framing structure at the juncture of the second floor and nearby walls, it is virtually impossible to distinguish a platform from a balloon frame. Era: After 1900.

The approximate age of a balloon or platform structure can be determined from the dimension of its lumber. Until the years just before World II, a two-by-four was actually 2 inches by 4 inches. However, in the years since, it has been 1 1/2 inches by 3 1/2 inches, 1/4 inch of each side having been planed off. Measure the rafters in your attic or joists in your basement. If the lumber is actually larger than the nominal dimension (say, 2 1/2 by 4 1/2 inches), the odds are the house is an early balloon frame, perhaps dating from the years just after the Civil War.

framing styles (the more common English forms differ from the Dutch style in numerous ways), all timber-frame houses have bents. Usually, the bents, made up of vertical posts and horizontal beams, form the end walls and divide the house into sections. In a house framed using the English system, the number of bents translates into a specific number of bays: a two-bent house has one bay, a three-bent house has two bays, and so on.

The size of a timber-frame building is traditionally measured by determining the number of bays it has. One theory has it that this method of measuring buildings resulted from

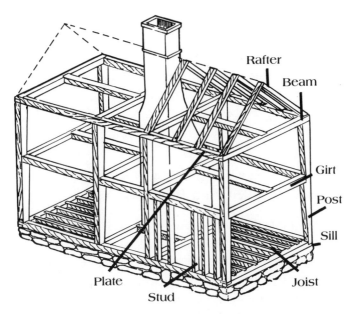

Rafter

Beam

Girt

Post

Sill

Plate

Stud

Joist

The early post-and-beam frame consisted of bents (which in turn were made up of vertical posts and horizontal girts and sills). The bents were tied together with horizontal "plates." Pairs of "rafters" angled upward from the plates, meeting in the middle to form the shape of the roof. This house consists of three bays (the chimney bay is at center, flanked by a bay on either side) defined by the four bents.

English feudalism, in which a serf was limited to one bay for every six acres of land he worked. In that agricultural era, it made for a sensible balance.

It is still useful to know the number of bays in a timber-frame house. A typical New England design has three bays (that is, four bents). There's a bent at each gable end, and a pair on either side of the center chimney. In between the first and second and the third and fourth bents are the windows; between the second and third is the door. A two-bay house would have a door in one bay, a window in the other, and would be, proportionately, one-third smaller. In medieval England, a bay was a standard length, about 16 feet long, or the distance required for two teams of oxen to stand side by side. That dimension varies greatly in American timber frames, but in early houses it is more likely to be honored than not.

17

The bents are connected to one another by horizontal pieces that run perpendicular to them. At the floor level this is the sill, but connecting the bents at the top of the posts are "plates." The floors are supported by wooden members called "joists." The rafters are tied together by "purlins." The last key element of the basic timber frame is the "brace," the diagonal members used to hold the building square.

THE LOG CABIN: A HISTORICAL MISUNDERSTANDING

For many years it was believed that early American houses were made of logs. The theory made sense: the trees had to be chopped down to clear the fields anyway, so why not just stack them into walls? There was even some evidence in New England that early fortifications had been built that way.

The notion that the log house was widespread in early America has now been abandoned, along with the idea that it was a peculiarly American building style. In fact, when Swedish settlers established the colony of New Sweden in 1638, in what is now Wilmington, Delaware, they brought with them a body of experience with log structures that dated back to the Mesolithic (Middle Stone) Age in Europe. Archaeologists believe that preagricultural peoples in today's Denmark, southern Sweden, and northern Germany built dwellings of assembled horizontal logs, with corners notched or even mortised. The Swedes and Finns who founded New Sweden used that same building technique to build their houses in North America. Unfortunately, there are but a few documented examples of Swedish log structures left.

The Swedes were the first to use the style for houses (unlike the English who adopted it for no more than an occasional stockade), but this type of construction gradually died out after the seizure of the Swedish colonies by the Dutch in 1655. Early in the eighteenth century a variation on the same theme was introduced by German settlers in Pennsylvania (they referred to themselves as "Deutsche," using their word for German, only to find themselves saddled with the misnomer "Pennsylvania Dutch"). Not all the German settlers built log houses, but those from such areas as the Black Forest, Silesia, and the Czech hills (including Bohemia and Moravia) had practiced this method of building on their home turf.

The frontier-style log cabin evolved largely from a style introduced by the German settlers. The English and Irish settlers quickly adopted it, as it was perfectly suited to pioneer life in the forests the settlers encountered as they went west. From Pennsylvania, Delaware, and southern New Jersey, the log house moved along the Ohio River valley and throughout the South, reaching as far as Texas and beyond. In Minnesota, Michigan, and Wisconsin, nineteenth-century Finnish immigrants also introduced log buildings, but they were rare in New York, New England, and the coastal colonies.

A "pen" is the basic unit of log cabin construction (the equivalent in a timber-frame house is a bay). It consists of four walls notched together at the corners, usually forming one room. Single-, double-, or triple-pen log houses are found. A log "cabin" is a single-pen structure with a dirt floor and stick-and-dirt chimney, but many log dwellings are a good deal more sophisticated. In colder climates, a double-pen house with a center chimney was typical (and often called a "saddlebag" house). In Texas and elsewhere in the South, the "dog-trot" configuration was popular; it consisted of two pens separated by an open passageway but covered by a single roof.

The log cabin could be quickly built: most went from standing timber to occupied dwelling within a month, perhaps even a matter of days if enough neighbors were available to help. As with a timber frame, the wood was cut locally and dragged to the site by horse or oxen. Depending upon the skills and time available, the tree trunks would be used round, split, or hewn flat for a tight fit. The quality of the hewing had a direct effect on the tightness of the building. The logs were then notched at the ends to join with those of the adjoining, perpendicular wall.

Usually openings for a door, windows (if any), or chimney

This 1847 woodcut illustrates a "dog-trot" log house, with its open passageway between the two rooms or "pens."

were cut after the logs were in place, and planks were affixed around the openings with wooden pins. The fireplace was of fieldstone, but its chimney was of wood cemented with clay. Chinks between the logs were filled with mud or clay, sometimes mixed with oak chips. By the turn of the nineteenth century, many log buildings were chinked with a lime-base cement. Hand-split shingles were the usual roofing materials.

Today, many sturdy log structures survive, most from the late eighteenth and early nineteenth centuries (on the frontier, log structures were common until about 1850). The stories of their discovery are legion, as their structures are often found hidden beneath modern sidings. Frequently one portion of a larger house is built of logs but is covered by a later, uniform exterior of clapboards, shingles, or stucco.

Tired of timbers and logs? Brick and stone houses were not unheard of in America's early settlements, though then, as now, wood was the rule. (We'll talk of brick and stone work in the next chapter.) But it is useful to have least a passing familiarity with the timber frame. Distinguishing it can help not only in identifying the ancient American house, but can put into perspective the life in those earlier eras by demonstrating how much work building was.

2.

LOOKING
ANEW AT
THE OLD

The single most important dating resource at your disposal is, of course, your house. A detailed physical examination of your house and property will reveal evidence of the past, both elements that are original and indications of what once was but has been removed or modified.

There are countless signs of the past in every older home, no matter how many remodelings it has experienced. Even if you have lived in the house for years, you must assume the critical detachment of one who is new to it. Psychologists are finding that we unconsciously screen out much more of the information offered our senses than we actually accept and process. No doubt, in living in your house, you have done that with many of its aspects. You've probably missed little clues in areas of the house you see every day. In rarely visited corners of the attic or other unused spaces, there may be even bigger ones waiting for you to discover.

The aim of this chapter is twofold: first, you will learn how and where to look for clues in and around your home; second, you will begin to learn how to assume the openness, the curiosity, and the perspicacity of the careful old-house investigator.

EXAMINING THE LOCATION

Unless your house was recently moved, its setting will offer clues about its evolution. The agricultural origins of a house can be identified by the tumble-down barns and sheds that surround it. A gracious Second Empire house (see page 115) amid a row of Victorian houses speaks for the nineteenth-century success of the town. Many such contextual conclusions are as easily drawn.

The Neighborhood: Where is the house and what's around it? Are the other buildings all residences or are (or were) some of them shops or stores? When the human foot or the horse hoof were the principal forms of locomotion, villages tended to be very compact, and the blacksmith shop, church, general store, and the majority of the dwellings were usually in the same vicinity. Outside the villages, satellite communities also developed. The impetus for their settlement varied, but before the industrial revolution, it was frequently the close proximity to sources of water power (for the all important saw-mill) or simply the crossing of two roads, which typically produced a "four-corners" hamlet. The school and church established in such outlying districts often served to provide a sense of community.

Try to identify patterns in the construction of neighboring houses. If the oldest house in the neighborhood is next door, it may well be a beacon for you in looking at old maps of your town and area. Identical houses all in a row suggest they were built at the same time by one developer while a heterogeneous collection implies a piecemeal, one-at-time construction pattern. If the house is in a row with identical Victorian structures, it may have been constructed by a mill owner as housing for his workers.

Try to establish the chronology. Within a well-developed town there are often earlier schemes to be observed. If your house is a tall, two-story affair amid Lilliputian ranches, it may be the old farmhouse whose substantial acreage was subsequently subdivided to accommodate the progeny of the fertile 1950s. In the post-World War II building boom, this occurred frequently.

By isolating the older houses, you may discover which roads were built first, and a pattern of development, planned or haphazard, may emerge. The railroad station became a focus for growth, so its presence (or absence) can explain neighborhood patterns. Often the best collections of older houses are in towns where the economy suddenly changed for the worse. The railroad bypassed the town, the mines dried up, or the highway was rerouted around the village. Growth and construction slowed or ceased, and the town fell into a time warp. Often it was the failure of the local mill that led to such a change of fortune.

The local historical society or library is the best place to pursue this sort of town history (see Chapter 6), but don't miss the clues that you can easily observe yourself. What's the street name? In the nineteenth century, most towns had an Elm Street. If your house is on Lincoln Street, chances are that the street was renamed or built after 1865. Check the maps at the town hall or historical society.

The Site: You may think you know every inch of your property, but take another look. If you have a survey or site plan of your lot, pull it out of your files, make a Xerox of it, and take it with you on your inspection. (Many banks require a survey before granting a mortgage, so chances are that one exists if you bought the house recently.)

Walk the boundaries of the property with the survey in hand. You are—here and elsewhere in your investigation—looking for any signs of the past.

On a property that was once a farm, chances are you'll find indications of fences—either stone walls or fence posts (watch out for old wires, they usually outlast their posts). In the Northeast, dense forests are often crisscrossed with stone walls. When the economy was agrarian, many hills and dales were deforested and cultivated or used for pasture. Everyone was a farmer, and everybody had a cow. But since the late nineteenth century, uncounted open fields have become forest floors.

Look, too, for rows of trees of evidently different vintage or variety from the rest. In a pine grove, several enormous maples suggest that at one time the maples were points of demarcation amid open fields and the fast-growing evergreens filled in when the farming stopped. A few unkempt apple trees may be the remnants of an orchard and could lead to a link with a will or inventory or some other paperwork clue. Look for old foundations, wells, graveyards, and old dumping grounds.

Old buildings on the property, whether their use is evident or unknown, can offer clues, too. If there is a stream or pond, add it—along with any other of these landmarks—to your map. Pace off distances to locate these sites on your map so that it approximates the actual property.

Don't forget to indicate the house on the survey, too. Sketch its approximate outline, to scale, in its correct position on the plot plan.

AMATEUR ARCHAEOLOGY

The new brick patio had taken him many back breaking hours, but he was proud of his handiwork. The patio made the large, private backyard a warm-weather escape.

Then, one winter day, the assembler of that patio walked across it, bound for his garage. Suddenly, he felt the earth move. Actually, the earth didn't move, but he and the patio did, following the pull of gravity. He found himself waist deep in an old cistern. Let's hope the same thing doesn't happen to you, but if it does, it may teach you much about your property.

Years ago, cisterns for catching and storing rainwater, which was then used for domestic chores, were common. When municipal water supplies became available and indoor plumbing commonplace, cisterns became unnecessary, and many were simply covered over.

Some of them, archaeologists have found, are full of artifacts. Thanks to gravity, it is possible to travel back through time, decade by decade. Since the notion of the landfill dump was still more than a century away, the cistern was an inviting target for tossing in small, usually broken, objects. What was dropped into a cistern in year one was buried beneath the detritus of year two, and so on, leaving behind a neatly chronological cache. Ceramics are frequently discovered in them (usually shards of broken plates). Other common artifacts include coins, photographs, bottles, old smoking pipes, and Indian beads.

While this book isn't about archaeology per se, the yards and immediate environs of many an old house will yield valuable objects. If your house predates the age of the machine, some archaeological digging may be particularly rewarding. Be forewarned that it's hard work and involves moving soil in substantial volumes. It's messy, too, of course.

Where to Look: Old wells and trash pits may contain clues of the life led nearby. When no longer used as water sources, old wells or cisterns were often converted to trash receptacles. The areas beneath porches, in crawl spaces under a house, and in the vicinity of old foundations are other good possibilities. Trash pits, too, may be excellent sources. Don't limit yourself to the immediate environs of the house, either, especially if it was a farmhouse. Walking in the Pennsylvania woods recently, I came up a steep slope about fifty yards behind (and out of sight of) an old farmhouse. The hillside was awash in old tin cans, abandoned gardening tools, and toys and rusty junk. What's beneath all that? It apparently hasn't been disturbed for decades, but the house dates from before 1780.

According to John Obed Curtis at Old Sturbridge Village, "A good spot to look for a household dump is just on the other side of the stone wall nearest to the house. Our forebears were not particularly fastidious about dumping household rubbish, even close to the house, and the closest repository was generally favored."

25

DON'T FORGET THE "NECESSARY HOUSE": If your old house has a small structure in the backyard that was once a privy or outhouse, don't overlook it out of squeamishness. When indoor plumbing made the privies unnecessary, they were often used for refuse. Even when functioning as a toilet, the privy was often the accidental recipient of objects lost or dropped into it. Today, long unused privies present no health risk, as the ordure has long since completely decomposed, in some cases leaving a wide variety of glass, ceramics, or metal objects for archaeologists to discover.

PRECAUTIONS: Old wells, even those dug by pick and shovel, can be 20, 30, 40, or more feet deep. So be careful when working in or near them. The material that seems to fill them may give way suddenly and settle some distance further down. Don't let it take you with it. Another thing: old stone walls that seem stable can give way at any time.

Documentation: Before removing any find from your diggings, make sure to record the depth and location where it was found. Context is all-important to such discoveries since the relation of one find to another (which item was beneath the other?) suggests chronology. After cleaning the object, you should bag, number, and label it. Careful drawings and plentiful photographs of the site will help you keep your findings organized.

THE GRID METHOD: Professional archaeologists divide up a site by roping off sections with stakes and twine. If you make a full-scale project of your digging, mark off sections that are large enough to work in but not so large that you lose the ability to locate your finds in context. Five-foot squares are workable.

PHOTOGRAPHS: Take pictures as you go, both of the objects found and the site. Be sure to include in the photos an object that indicates scale. Although a ruler is best, any familiar object, like a glove or paper cup, will do.

SIZING UP THE BUILDING

Begin with a relaxed inspection of the outside. The point here is to see the forest despite the trees. Stand a short distance, perhaps fifty yards, away from the house. It may help if you squint slightly, so you see less detail and more form.

Try to separate the place into parts. Is there one main volume surrounded by others? Is there a simple shed addition that quite obviously was added later? Can you see what once was a simple symmetrical building that has been rendered otherwise by additions? Perhaps the single best exterior clue to the floor plan of a building is its doorway. If it's in the center, then there is most likely a symmetrical arrangement of rooms on either side of the center hall or center chimney. In an older house, however, chances are the floor plan today is not exactly what it was when the house was built.

Look for evidence of new partitions inside: they may have been added or removed. Closets and bathrooms may have been inserted. And that's before considering any additions.

A door of a different style from those found elsewhere may indicate change. Different moldings may also be observed, but keep in mind that in many houses the moldings around doors and windows (architraves) are simplified from the first to the second floor. Sometimes a chair rail or other molding will be found in a closet, suggesting that the interior of the closet was once part of the room. Look for patterns of wear on the floor where a door used to be.

There may be patch marks or outlines evident on the walls or ceilings where partitions were removed. Hairline cracks in straight lines are generally the result of changes rather than settlement and indicate doors or windows that were covered up in a remodeling. Kitchens and bathrooms are virtually guaranteed to have been substantially changed.

Style: Identifying the style of your house is important to determining the age of its construction and to understanding the life in the house in its earlier era. Making that determination requires a careful examination of the house, both close up and from afar.

What is the ratio of the length to the width? Is the roofline simple, with but one ridge, or are there dormers? Is it a hip or pyramidal roof? Look at the arrangement of the windows: Are they all aligned? Does only one break the pattern, or is the arrangement seemingly haphazard?

You may already have determined the style of your house. If you haven't, the Style Notes in Chapters 3, 4, and 5 should help you resolve that question. If you still aren't sure, keep in mind that many houses built for the middle class weren't adorned with the details of more expensive high-style homes. In many areas, a popular configuration—like Greek Revival in rural New England or a variation of American Gothic in the mid-Atlantic states—would outlast its period. Sometimes,

Identifying the type of roof on your house may be important to recognizing its style. A mansard roof, for example, almost certainly indicates the house was built in the Second Empire style in the second half of the nineteenth century. Other shapes are characteristic of other styles, as the Style Notes in the following chapters explain.

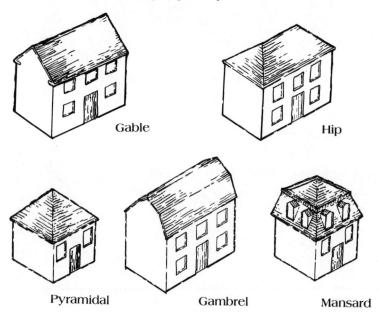

Gable

Hip

Pyramidal

Gambrel

Mansard

the original trim would be abandoned, making the house simpler; in other cases, new decorative details were added to the older shapes the builders knew best. In any case, older houses have often lost much exterior detail. Probably far more gingerbread has been taken to junk heaps than remains in place in areas of the United States with cold, wet climates, thanks to both the weather and the installers of vinyl and aluminum sidings.

In investigating your house, be alert for remaining detail. That one remaining piece of bargeboard on the bay window or the pointed-arch window says American Gothic, even if all the rest of the detail is gone. Such indications should send you scurrying to learn more about that style. In doing so, you may wish to refer to a style manual. (The most comprehensive is Virginia and Lee McAlester's *A Field Guide to American Houses*. It devotes some forty chapters and more than 1,200 photos to helping make such determinations. See For Further Reading for information about the McAlesters' and other style books).

Additions: Buildings are not organic, yet they do have a definite life of their own. A building changes to reflect the lives of those who live in it, mirroring changes as families expand or contract and good fortune comes and goes. Social trends are also manifest in house changes. Attached garages began to appear in the 1920s; they were obligatory after 1950. Technology had its effects, too, making available the new and different and, sometimes, the improved. To a house, as to any organism, change is the order of things.

In the South, a common house configuration that has evolved over the generations is referred to as "big house, little house, colonnade, and kitchen." The little house came first, perhaps in the eighteenth century. The big house came later, after the farm was successful and the owner could afford to build a larger, grander home. The kitchen was a summer kitchen, separated from the house so the heat of cooking in the summer wouldn't make the house hotter than it already was.

In the North, a similar configuration is known as "big house, little house, back house, and barn." While all four parts were often built simultaneously (usually in the mid-nineteenth century), the arrangement of the structures was the result of practical considerations. The back house was likely to be a woodshed or other utility building (with the privy built in), and it linked the barn to the kitchen that dominated the little house. The main house had a parlor and dining room downstairs and bedrooms above. On a cold winter day in New England, the farmer appreciated being able to avoid walking across the barnyard in order to milk his cows.

When you are studying your house, chances are the separation of sections won't be as evident as in these arrangements, but you must determine if there were later additions. Remodelings are important, too. The older a house is, the greater the chances that it has been added on to. The changes that can most easily be seen from the exterior include ells, shed additions, and dormers.

Often the best single clues to additions are things that

Houses like the one in this ca. 1925 photo (note the Ford Model A) have come to be called "big house, little house, back house, and barn." Found all over New England, this configuration suited the integrated work and family life of the small farmer. The barn was the dairy. The big house at the front held the public spaces, with bedrooms upstairs. In between were the woodshed, kitchen, and sometimes even the privy.

don't fit: if all the doors in the house are the same but one; if the brickwork matches everywhere but in one spot; if the clapboards are all equally weathered except in one area.

How about the windows: Are those in one section different from the rest? A late Victorian addition, for example, might have 2/2 sashes while those in the original Georgian structure might be 9/6s or 12/8s. In both wood and masonry homes, look for signs that windows or doors have been closed off. Note any windows that seem to be in odd places. Windows jammed in a corner may indicate that a wall was added. A window that is shaped differently from the rest or that breaks up an otherwise symmetrical arrangement may once have been a decorative window, perhaps a stained-glass window that got broken or was replaced.

Usually, patched walls reveal themselves by an irregular pattern of bricks or siding slotted into the fabric of the older wall.

Is there a vertical board in the middle of a clapboard surface? Such a board probably started life as a corner board, meaning that at one time it stood at the end of the wall.

Does the pitch of the roof change? If the roof is a gambrel, then there will be matched changes in pitch on the front and back of the house; otherwise, a change in pitch suggests an addition.

If the walls are masonry, is there an apparent change in materials or is there an evident vertical joint where the new joins the old? Does the mortar between the bricks or stones change color from one section to the next? Does the detailing change at some point? Is one section sided in one material and the rest in another? If no such changes are visible, that doesn't assure that no additions were made, as the entire house could well have been resided and reroofed at some point in the house's history, obscuring the old lines of demarcation.

In such cases, foundations can be a good indicator of the serial nature of the construction of a house. If part of it has a fieldstone foundation while another is supported by concrete blocks, chances are the portion over the blocks was built well after the stone section. Look at the roof, too. A seam in a roof suggests an addition, as does an otherwise healthy roof with a noticeable sag in one spot. A visible sag at the center of an early New England house may mean that a large, center chimney stack was removed. This can be confirmed by examining the area from the inside, where the one-time exit hole for the masonry stack has been framed in and boarded over with materials quite different from the rest of the framing.

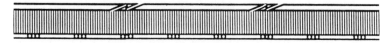

WATCHING
THE WINDOWS

A 9/6 window in an eighteenth-century house.

Windows: Windows can be invaluable clues to determining the age and style of a house. The key identifying characteristics of windows are as follows:

CONFIGURATIONS: 12/12 (that is, twelve-over-twelves, windows with twelve panes or lights in the

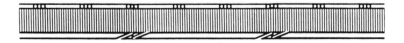

upper sash and twelve more in the lower one), 12/8, 9/9, 9/6: common in the eighteenth century; 6/6: dominant from the late eighteenth century until about 1850; 2/2: the norm for the second half of the nineteenth century; 1/1: common from the late nineteenth century on. However, during the Colonial Revival, Sears and other retailers sold multilight sashes, 6/6 and 6/1 being the most popular.

SASH WEIGHTS: Until about 1850 most sash windows had fixed top sashes. The lower sash slid up and down and had to be pinned or braced open. Double-hung, sash-weighted windows became dominant thereafter.

GLASS: Handmade glass (distinguished by curved waves, bubbles, and other imperfections) was usual until about 1880. In general, the least perfect glass was used in out-of-the-way places: for attic sashes, windows in servants' rooms, or in barns. Decorative stained-glass windows post-date 1880.

The availability of relatively inexpensive glass (and thus replacement sashes) in the mid-nineteenth century and after led to a wholesale replacement of windows (a trend that continues to this day, in fact). In the Victorian age, 2/2s came to be the norm both for new construction and for the "rehabilitation" of older homes. Unfortunately for those intent upon restoring the original look to a Colonial house, not only the window sashes but the frames as well were often replaced to install the sash weight systems.

The enormous, single-pane "picture window" is a post-World War II introduction.

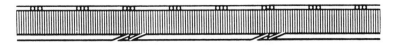

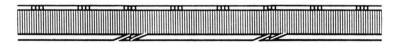

Shutters and Blinds: The earliest shutters were solid boards; the Dutch were using paneled shutters by 1720. As the popularity of Georgian houses spread, so did louvered blinds with moldings; the louvers didn't move. That innovation didn't come till about 1835. (Technically, louvered shutters are "blinds.")

In New England, shutters were located inside rather than outside the window until the late eighteenth century. (But in the mid-Atlantic states and southern New England, exterior shutters and blinds were to be found during that period.) The interior shutters provided privacy, since curtains were unusual because of the expensiveness of cloth. Since that era, however, exterior shutters have remained largely in vogue, despite some ups and downs in popularity (the Colonial Revival being a notable high point).

Many "shutters" are merely excrescences added in order to "colonialize" houses. In general, this is the case if they don't work (that is, if there are no hinges and the shutters are nailed or screwed to the siding of the house); if they are the wrong size (that is, they are not large enough to cover the windows to which they are attached); or if they are only half there (as often happens with shutters added to houses not designed for them, where windows are located so close together that the shutters don't have sufficient space to sit flat to the side of the house).

Shape: Once you have decided which portion of the house was the original core, consider its shape. In determining the style and much else about the house, it's important to be able to distinguish whether the original house was one or two rooms deep (see discussions of single- and double-pile construction, page 75).

Is the front door on a side wall or a gable end? With the coming of the Greek influence, the gable-end arrangement became popular. Is the entry in the center and are the windows symmetrically arranged? If not, then the house probably postdates 1825 or so when the previous styles—all of which were basically symmetrical—were joined by asymmetrical ones.

Is the house one, one-and-a-half, or two stories tall? That is, is there living space only on the first floor (a single-story design), or does the second floor have rooms with ceilings defined by the pitch of the roof (the one-and-a-half configuration), or does the second story have full ceilings?

Check the chimney arrangement. Is there only one in the center or are there two, either one on each of the end walls or asymmetrically located? Is the chimney massive (two feet or

One-Story House

One-and-a-Half-Story House

Two-Story House

more square at the roof line and several times that at the base) or comparatively spindly? The smaller chimney indicates either a chimney replacement or that the house was designed for later (post-1830) heating methods such as stoves or furnaces. If the chimney(s) is (are) not located symmetrically, it (they) may also be a clue that a later section was added to one end or the other of the structure.

The Porch: Approach the house, studying the trim and other details. Do all the surfaces seem of a piece, or is a change apparent? On clapboard houses that date from the Victorian era, you'll often see that clapboards have been replaced in one section between the first- and second-story windows. That usually means there was a porch that began to decay and the decision was made to remove rather than repair it. The point at which it joined the structure of the house was then reclapboarded. The careful eye can detect that a few courses of clapboards have a smoother surface than the rest, with fewer layers of paint.

If there is a porch, does it appear to be of a piece or has it been doctored? A heavy wooden cornice supported by a slight, wrought-iron railing and posts suggests that the original wooden superstructure was replaced. Look for signs of the original posts on the floor of the porch or siding of the house where they would have been attached. Old nail holes or paint patterns may also indicate the change.

Foundations: A stone foundation means something, as does the presence or absence of mortar. Concrete block foundations, too, can be "read" to indicate time.

Foundations vary from one part of the country to another. In the North, because winter frost penetrates more deeply, cellars are deeper. Foundations also vary by age. Though early houses have often had their original foundations enlarged or rebuilt over the years, the rule in general is the earlier the house, the less cellar one is likely to find. After all, the steam shovel and backhoe didn't appear until the nineteenth and twentieth centuries, and digging enormous holes in the ground with a shovel is hard work.

The French architecture of New Orleans is now virtually extinct because of the effect of wet and soft soil on foundations. Wood was used at first, but that rotted away. When brick became available, that too failed because the soft soil led to settlement cracks and the moisture to deteriorating bricks. Only a handful of New Orleans houses from the eighteenth century have survived to our time.

Fieldstone (that is, random stone found in fields) is the rule in the North. Fields that have been cultivated since the seventeenth century still seem to grow rocks as each year the frost produces a few from the depths. The glacier dragged them along eons ago, and farmers have been removing them ever since they arrived. It is the plentifulness of fieldstone that explains the fondness for stone foundations.

In other parts of the country, brick is more common. Unlike stone which was often laid dry, brick is always laid with mortar. Look carefully at the bricks: Are they consistent in shape and texture, indicating that they are machine-made, or are there irregularities in the surface and shape that suggest they were handmade? Machine-made brick dates from no earlier than the second half of the nineteenth century.

In the last quarter of the nineteenth century, concrete came into use, but poured concrete or concrete block wasn't the rule until the twentieth century. At about the same time, a false stone made of concrete also came into use. If the "stones" of your foundation are all exactly the same size and have the texture of concrete, that's the explanation.

Examine all parts of the foundation, inside and out. If it's all stone, it probably predates our century. If it's concrete, chances are it's of twentieth-century construction. However, if it is stone on the inside and concrete on the outside, the explanation probably is that a previous owner of the house, grown tired of a wet basement, faced the exterior with a layer of cement to seal it.

In general, a foundation can be seen as a clear indication

of the age of a house. However, when a house is moved, an all-new undercarriage is usually added. If you find a modern foundation beneath an old house, that could be the explanation.

Siding: What is the siding? Clapboards, shingle, brick, stucco, or stone? If the siding of the house is aluminum (detected by the metallic ping it makes when tapped with a fingertip), vinyl (it flexes when touched), asphalt shingles (an asphalt-impregnated medium like fiberglass coated with sand-like granules), or asbestos shingles (a thin, brittle, textured material), it may obscure much evidence as to the age of the house. An older siding is likely to be beneath, unless the house was built in the years after World War II, when all of these sidings became popular.

CLAPBOARDS: On seventeenth- and eighteenth-century houses, lower clapboards were sometimes closer together than those higher on the walls, though this was by no means a standard practice. Until circular-sawn clapboards came into general use after 1830, most clapboards were aproximately 4 to 6 feet in length. On houses built since then, lengths are generally longer. Look for joints between pieces to make this determination.

Look a second time at the joints between pieced clapboards. Were the boards cut at a 90-degree angle to the surface of the clapboard (to make a "butt" joint) or were they tooled at an angle to make an overlapping "scarfe" joint? Scarfe joints were often used before 1825, but after that date butt joints became the usual method.

SHINGLES AND SHAKES: In the eighteenth century, roof or sidewall shingles were split from pine, cypress or other woods and tooled smooth with a drawknife. The finished product was quite regular, with a uniform taper. Roofing shingles were often longer (perhaps 36 inches in length), while shingles used for a siding surface were more likely to be 18 inches or 24 inches in length.

The word "shingle" is used broadly in nineteenth-century and earlier sources. In today's terminology, the word "shake"

On the gable of this Queen Anne house is a deceptively simple blend of two shingle shapes together with complementary decorations on the frieze, verge board, and window frame. All these elaborations were products of steam-powered machinery.

most often refers to the thick, irregularly textured shingles that are *split* from the wood (in contrast to shingles which are sawed) and left with a highly textured surface. These hefty, exaggerated shakes really aren't appropriate for the restoration of nineteenth-century or earlier houses.

As steam-powered machinery came into use in the mid-nineteenth century, shingles suddenly afforded the builder a wide range of decorative options, including rounded, pointed, fish-scale, and other shapes. Two or more types were often used in alternating courses, commonly on gables, turrets or mansard roofs.

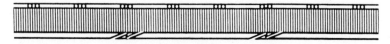

PAINT
CHRONOLOGIES

Virtually all old houses have an accretion of layers of paint. On the exterior of an eighteenth-century house, it is not unusual to find twenty-five coats. Sometimes the accumulation of paint is so thick on the inside that the moldings have lost their definition. The paint may also have cracked (checking or alligatoring are other words for the same thing).

Regardless of the number of layers of paint, you may wish to know what the original or other, early paint schemes were. A simple set of procedures can help you determine the "paint chronology" of your house.

Where to Work: On the exterior of the house, find a place that has been least exposed to the weather. On the interior, select a unobtrusive location in case your patchwork afterward is less than perfect. It may be necessary to investigate both the flat surfaces of the wall and the nearby moldings, as they are likely to have been painted different, complementary colors.

Keep in mind that old pigments were often unstable, so they have faded. Oil paint also yellows, so the colors may seem darker now than when ap-

BRICK: In previous centuries, bricks differed, depending upon who made them. Today's standard brick is roughly the size of the early English-style brick, about 2 1/2 inches tall, 8 inches long, and 4 inches wide. But Dutch brick was thinner,

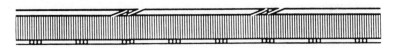

plied. In general colors were probably somewhat brighter than the paint chronology suggests.

Paint Removal Methods: You may need to use all of the following three methods of scraping to determine what came before.

THE SCRAPER METHOD: On flat surfaces, using a narrow paint scraper (1 to 2 inches wide), scrape back and forth. Be sure to hold the tool perpendicular to the surface being investigated in order to prevent gouging. It may take time, patience, and elbow grease, but gradually a story will emerge. Stop at regular intervals and inspect your scraping, especially at the edge, with a magnifying glass.

THE SCALPEL METHOD: This is helpful when trying to penetrate many layers of paint on a smaller piece of wood, like a strip of molding. Use a sharp utility or X-Acto knife. Holding it at about a 60-degree angle to the wood, carefully cut a small conical hole in the wood. (It shouldn't be more than about three-eighths of an inch in diameter so that wood filler can be used to patch it later.) A magnifying glass will reveal the layers of paint.

SANDPAPER METHOD: Another option is to use fine sandpaper. Working in a circular motion in a two- or three-inch arc, you can create a "bull's eye" that will reveal all the layers of the paint.

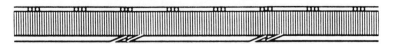

standing only about 1 1/2 inches high. The Dutch used all of the bonds cited below, as well as bricks with different shades of glaze, including red, pink, orange, yellow, and even purple, for patterned, geometric effect.

By 1830, virtually all bricks were of the standard size used since. Today, brick-makers often stamp their names on the tops of bricks before they are baked. The name is then covered with mortar when the building is built. If in the process of demolition you come across bricks with names stamped in them, it is likely that the brick—and probably the building— dates from the mid-nineteenth century or after.

The long side of a brick is called a "stretcher," the end a "header." A horizontal row of bricks is a "course." The arrangement of bricks in a wall—that is, the "bond"—can be an indication of age.

English Bond: The typical pattern of brickwork in the seventeenth century was English bond, in which header and stretcher courses alternated (though in some cases, there are two or three or even more stretcher courses between headers, and the bond is still termed "English.") English bond was also popular during the Federal period (see page 87) for masonry houses.

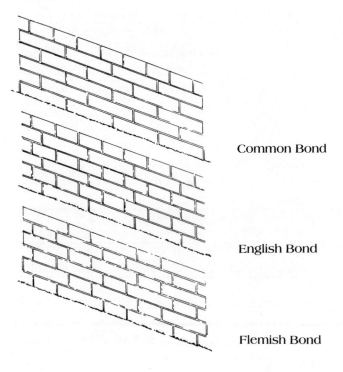

Common Bond

English Bond

Flemish Bond

Flemish Bond: After the turn of the eighteenth century and also for Federal-style houses Flemish bond, in which headers and stretchers alternated within each course, became more common. This bond was usual in Georgian houses (see page 85).

Common or American Bond: In American bond, all courses are made only of stretchers. This is the most common method of bricklaying used today, and is also sometimes called "running bond."

Roofing Materials: There are no original roofs left from the eighteenth century except for the worn-out residue sometimes found beneath later surfaces. If remnants of old shingles are found, check the nails. The use of wrought nails dates the house as earlier than 1800 (see discussion of nail dating, page 54). Many houses have roofs that date from the nineteenth century. Their surfaces are either slate or tin.

TIN-PLATED ROOFING: Tin was available in the seventeenth century, but it was expensive, since all tin came from England. Until the turn of the nineteenth century, its roofing applications were usually confined to "leaders" linking the gutters and downspouts.

After 1800, the material termed "tin"—which was actually thin sheets of iron dipped into a bath of molten tin that left it coated with a layer of tin—became one of the householder's best friends. It came in sheets (10 inches by 14 inches and 20 inches by 14 inches were common sizes) and was used for making everything from pots and pans to tin roofing and gutters.

In the early decades of the century, tin-plated roofs called "terne" roofs (made of sheet iron coated with an alloy of lead and tin) began to appear on the houses of wealthy city dwellers. By the 1840s, the countryside, too, was dotted with terne-roofed houses. The material continued to be used for the rest of the century and still is today, though infrequently. Since tin roofs must be primed and painted, the range of colors is unlimited, though they were often painted red. (Beware, how-

THE DATING
OF DATES

As if the temple front of this pretty little Greek Revival house in Essex, New York, didn't telegraph its age, there's a date, too, on the frieze board.

A Connecticut couple was thrilled to find the figures 1716 carved in a beam in their old house. When the town historian told them that according to a 1725 map there was no house on that property, they were confused.

They learned later from an old letter and bills found in a trunk in the barn that some of the main

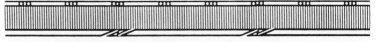

ever, when painting tin roofs of using asphalt-based roof paint. When wet, it will create sulfuric acid and deteriorate the tin.)

Tin roofs generally have seams that run down the pitch of a roof. The separate pieces in each run are soldered together

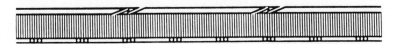

structural members had been salvaged from another house that had been destroyed in a storm. So, yes, some of the house was from 1716, but its true date was actually a good deal later.

Be happy if you find dates in your house—but you don't believe *everything* you read, do you? The year inscribed may indeed be that of construction, but it may also be the date of an addition or of a major renovation. It may even be the date of a wedding, added to welcome the wife to the yeoman's home.

Look for dates carved and scrawled on beams or other wooden members. There may be explanations, too, along the lines of "This ell added in 18—" or "Roof replaced by Carpenter John Atkinson in 17—." In many Pennsylvania stone houses, there are date panels, usually set in a visible location, either inside or out. As a general rule, dates on large, difficult-to-move stones (on exterior quoins or lintels over the fireplace or door) are more likely to be genuine than those in a brick or a single, small stone that could have been inserted at almost any time.

Beware of dates that come via previous owners. Dating a house involves corroborating evidence: when dealing with nineteenth-century or earlier houses, no one source should be taken as authoritative.

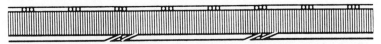

to form a roll; the lengths are then extended from the peak of the roof downward, and the joints between the lengths are fastened at a seam formed by folds in the edge of the sheets. The resulting seam is known as a "standing seam." In some cases, the long seams are also soldered, producing a "flat seam" that sits almost flush with the roof surface. Metal roofing is easily distinguished by the metallic ping produced by tapping on it. (Note, however, that sheet-metal roofs with a corrugated surface date from the twentieth century.)

SLATE: Slate is a type of stratified rock that is generally red or gray. The earliest slate in America used as a roofing material was thick, roughly ⅝ inch to ¾ inch thick. However, by the Civil War, when railroads made shipping the heavy materials easier, the popularity of slate spread, too, and by then it was the more standard, thinner slate we still see today that was being used. Typically, slate shingles are about a quarter-inch thick, but they vary greatly in width and length.

WOOD: Wood roofing shingles are nailed to a wooden framework laid across the roof parallel to the ridge. Typically in New England, this sub-roof would be of wide, rough-cut boards, while further south it was more likely to be of more numerous, narrower wooden strips. Gaps were left between the sub-roof boards (several inches with the narrow strips, an inch or less with the wider boards) so that the underside of the shingles could "breathe" when they expanded and contracted as water alternately was absorbed and evaporated. The ventilation facilitated the process.

Hand-split shakes will last up to fifty years as a roofing surface, shingles perhaps a bit more than half that. As a result, a shingle or shake roof found today is almost certain to date from no earlier than the Depression years.

One small dating trick for the pre-1850 house is to examine the sub-roof from inside the attic. (The sub-roof is composed of the boards that run across the rafters beneath the actual surface of the roof.) If the edges of those boards were not cut square—if they vary with the contours of the tree from which they were sawn—the house probably predates 1850. Most boards were trimmed straight after that date, even for secondary uses like sub-roofs. (To make matters complicated, however, virtually all houses with tin roofs, even those predating 1850, have sub-roofs made of boards that were trimmed

46

square. The likely explanation is that if people had enough money for a tin roof, they could pay for a more precisely finished sub-roof as well.)

Exterior Trim: Intricately cut bargeboards or other gingerbread suggest a house is Victorian. However, many earlier houses were "updated" in the nineteenth century, and, in recent years, gingerbread has had a revival, so its presence is no guarantee of a nineteenth-century house. Examine the trim as closely as possible: Is there evidence of layers of paint? Are pieces broken off? Is there evident decay?

Look at the architrave moldings around the windows and doors. Georgian and Greek Revival houses have characteristic doorways (see page 77). Are there quoins at the corners? How about pilasters? Is there a fancy entry with sidelights or a fan sash? The door itself may be a clue, too, as may be the windows. Be sure not to miss the little indications that may signify style or alterations. It is always important to balance your observations. Since individual elements like the front door may have been changed to "update" a building, take it as one piece of evidence and try and support your conclusions about it with other evidence.

REGIONALITY

What was stylish in Philadelphia in 1815 wasn't built for a decade or more only twenty-five miles west. In the Northeast, the medieval-inspired houses of Colonial New England design went out of fashion after the Revolution, but in Ohio, many "Connecticut farmhouses" were still being built thirty or more years later. When new settlements were being established miles away from the then trendy towns, the builders reverted to the old ways, tools, and materials. They built what they knew rather than what was in vogue.

The apprenticeship tradition also remained an important factor throughout the eighteenth and nineteenth centuries. Young men learning from older master builders might well be taught techniques and technologies of an earlier era, and many of the practices of the past were passed on in this fashion. However, as labor-saving devices and new ideas appeared, they were also adopted.

An intensive study of other buildings in a town or region is essential to establishing with certainty when a style or building practice came or ceased to be used in a given vicinity. Trends differed from area to area, but after about 1830 most of the major ones were adopted nationally. There are time lapses between the adoption of the new in older, established cultural centers and in communities located far from these centers, just as today styles generally move outward from New York or Los Angeles, and reach Idaho after San Francisco. The difference is the length of time that elapses. Information that, in our time, takes weeks or months to transmit might, in eighteenth-century America, have taken decades to travel the same distances.

Now that you've started your scrutiny of your house, you've begun the process of discovery. It takes time, especially in a house that has seen much renovation over the decades, to develop the sort of second sight you need to put your house into its historical perspective. Only gradually does one develop a deeper understanding of a house. Sometimes observations made over a period of months will suddenly fit together, offering a surprising revelation about what was changed, or perhaps why. Allow yourself the chance to absorb what you have learned in your search and what living in the house teaches you.

3.

THE
HANDMADE
HOUSE

1630–1830

I must have been about seven years old. We were traveling from my home in Massachusetts to New York State. "There's the border," my mother said, pointing out the sign that read "Welcome to New York."

I looked intently out the car window. I knew from studying maps what borders looked like—they were usually dotted lines—but as hard as I tried I couldn't discern any such markings on the terrain we passed by. When I asked my parents for clarification, they seemed to find the whole matter very entertaining indeed.

In a sense, writing history involves a similar kind of mapping, assigning dotted lines to the terrain of history. Locating those boundaries is often arbitrary, as the historian tries to make sense of an experience he hasn't had and can never have. For the historian and his audience, labels and dates must delimit eras and movements, making comprehensible widely varied experiences.

Architectural history is no exception. It's filled with approximations and guesswork, attempts to establish a parallel printed universe that re-creates in our minds the ways in which buildings came to be. In this chapter and the two that follow, we will review in brief the evolution of the American house, both in terms of style and of the materials and tools used to build it. This history is divided by a pair of lines of demarcation. While these lines are about as arbitrary as the 38th parallel was to the Koreas, they provide a useful way of comprehending a large and diverse body of information.

The "handmade" house comes first. It predates the years during which the impact of the industrial revolution became widespread. Until the advent of new methods of cutting wood (using power saws with circular blades) and of fastening it together (with inexpensive, machine-made nails), most house parts were made by the carpenter, often on site and usually by hand.

Thus, for our purposes in dating and identifying houses, the first major dividing line in American architectural history is ca. 1830. The transition involved more than nails and saws, as much machinery was developed that produced manufactured goods in volume, and the all-important railroad system developed, making the delivery of those goods possible and affordable. In construction terms, that industrial evolution led to the disappearance of the handmade. By 1850, little of the wood used to construct a typical house was shaped by the human hand, but owed its configuration to the machine.

While these changes came at a cost of some of the individual character that a talented craftsman was required to invest in his work, it also meant a wider range of decorative details was possible. The Victorian era, which takes its name from the English queen whose reign conveniently (but almost irrelevantly) extended from 1837 to 1901, featured wildly varied stylistic experimentation, from the American Gothic to the elaborately decorated Queen Anne. These experiments were made possible by the machine, and it is the very diversity of Victorian houses that best characterizes this second major era of American architectural history, the subject of Chapter 4, "The Victorian House."

The second key boundary divides the Victorian from the twentieth-century house. It is less a mechanical matter than one of style. While in the eclectic Victorian age the American house assumed at various times passing resemblances to ancient Greek temples, Gothic cathedrals, Renaissance palaces, and medieval European townhouses, by the turn of the twentieth century, American buildings began to look to American sources rather than European ones. The Prairie style house and the bungalow are peculiarly American dwellings, while the houses that belong to the Colonial Revival cast glances backward at earlier, *American* houses. Thus, it is a self-consciously American quality that distinguishes the houses of the early twentieth century from the Victorian experiments that preceded them.

The handmade house is the subject of this chapter, including the Cape Cod house, the saltbox, the early houses of the Dutch and the Spanish settlers, and houses built in the Georgian and the Federal styles. (The Federal style, which is also known as Adamesque, and the similar Georgian configuration are perhaps better known as "Colonial.") In Chapter 4, the houses of the years ca. 1830–1900 will take center stage, while Chapter 5 brings us into the first third of our own century.

We begin with a little time travel.

A MATTER OF CHOICE

For the homeowner building a house today, among the most time-consuming aspects of the job is the decision-making. There are hundreds of available faucets for a shower: Which do you like? What about doors and windows and cabinets and floors and fixtures and appliances? How big, how expensive, what color, what materials, from which supplier? If we choose this, then what about that . . .? Whether it's a light fixture or the bathroom tile, thousands of *choices* have to be made.

If choice is today's challenge, it certainly wasn't yesterday's. Until railroads made it possible to ship a wide range of goods, builders were dependent upon local materials. The timber for the frame was often made from trees felled on the property. The boards needed were usually cut at the sawmill in town. In fact, until after 1830, the establishment of a sawmill usually meant that a community would come to exist nearby.

Until after 1800, virtually all nails were made by hand. Iron rods roughly a quarter-inch thick and several feet long were prefabricated by blacksmiths. Called "nail rods," they were used by many an average farmer who, during spare winter hours, would heat and hammer out the nails he required for warm-weather building projects or a few extra dollars. The results of his labors were hand-wrought nails, distinguished by their large heads (often as large as ½ inch in diameter) which bore the evidence of their manufacture. (Several hammer strokes were required to make the head, producing a roselike shape and resulting in the nickname "rose-head" nails.)

The price of nails was so significant that to this day the terminology used to identify their size is an expression of their price. One hundred nails of a certain size cost three pennies, so they were referred to as "three-penny nails"; the next size up was termed "four-penny," and so on. In Colonial Virginia in 1645, the value of nails was recognized in another way. An ordinance was put into effect prohibiting the burning down of buildings to salvage the nails used in their construction.

Paint, too, was often made at home. Milk was used as a base. Soil with traces of iron was burned to produce the pigment used to make the popular "Venetian-red" paint. Lampblack was another common pigment.

Shingles for roofs, stone for foundations, were all local. The paneling, moldings, or other decorative woodwork were not only likely to be made of local goods, but were most likely to have been shaped by hand by the carpenter himself. Not surprisingly, these hand-shaped materials help give the earliest houses their character.

While limitations of transportation were less of an issue in major cities like Boston, New York, Philadelphia, and Baltimore with their fine harbors and flourishing shipping trades, the peculiar fact is that relatively little trading occurred between colonies, though trade with Europe was commonplace throughout the seventeenth and eighteenth centuries. Trade with inland towns was also limited. After the American Revolution, interstate trade began to grow, but both before and after the war high-quality manufactured goods were expensive and largely the province of the wealthy.

As a result, dollars and cents were also a key limitation in constructing houses. Except for certain relatively crude items crafted by local blacksmiths, virtually all hardware (hinges and latches) was brought from abroad, England in particular. The same was true of glass, high-style furniture, and other goods. As a result these and the other materials that had to be purchased were kept at a minimum. Today, of course, the economics of building is the reverse: virtually no component part is made by the builder on site, since that would render it too expensive; everything is brought in from all over the globe, down to such raw materials as lumber and boards.

Obtaining a smooth board in the seventeenth or eighteenth century involved an investment of time and skilled labor. A rough-cut board had to be planed by hand. It was a two-step process, beginning with a flat-bottomed wooden plane with a slightly curved iron blade, called a "jack plane," which eliminated the roughness and evidence of the saw cuts. A second plane, called a "smoothing plane," was used to give the boards a smooth-to-the-eye appearance.

Note that they were made smooth-to-the-eye rather than smooth-to-the-touch. The blade on the smoothing plane also had a slight arc (though much less of one than on the jack plane). As a result hand-planed boards are not machine-flat like the boards that are produced by a mill today. When you run your fingers across the grain of a hand-planed board, you can feel its contours. This is an invaluable trick in identifying early planed paneling, floor boards, door panels, and other wood elements.

Learning to distinguish hand-planned surfaces takes only

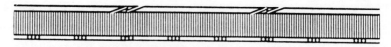

KNOWING YOUR NAILS

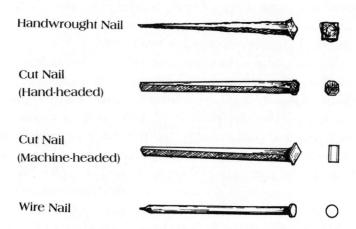

Handwrought Nail

Cut Nail
(Hand-headed)

Cut Nail
(Machine-headed)

Wire Nail

Handwrought Nails: Handwrought nails were the rule until the end of the eighteenth century. They have square or rectangular shanks, and were pointed and headed by hammering. After the turn of the nineteenth century, they were used only in limited applications, so any house in which handwrought nails were used to attach the sheathing or interior trim almost certainly predates 1800. Era: until ca. 1800.

Cut Nails: The first known cut-nail machine in the United States was patented in 1789. It produced cut nails that had no heads. The first cut nails, however, had handmade heads, usually distinguished by a narrowing of the nail just before the head (at the "neck"), which was a result of the way the nail

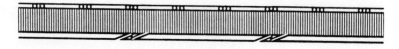

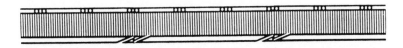

was pinched in a viselike device during the heading process. The shaft of all cut nails was rectangular and tapered. Era: cut nails with handmade head, after 1790 until ca. 1825.

Though first manufactured about 1815, machine-headed cut nails weren't produced in quantity until the 1820s. By then the heads were more nearly regular. Because earlier cut nails were headed manually, their heads bore indications of the irregular hammer strokes; on the other hand, the machine-headed cut nails had flat heads. By 1830, the process of nail cutting had been refined to the degree that the cut nails made then are virtually indistinguishable from those made today. Era: Cut nails with machine heads were used as an all-purpose nail ca. 1825 to 1890, and were used for flooring and masonry purposes from ca. 1825 to the present.

Wire Nails: Wire nails have round shafts. A very early variety was used in England in the 1790s in furniture- and box-making, but it wasn't until after 1870 that American factories produced them for building purposes. Initially, only smaller sizes were available (they began to be widely used to fasten moldings by about 1880), but it wasn't until the late 1880s that they truly began to compete with the cut nails. As late as 1886, more than 90 percent of the nails manufactured in the United States were cut nails, but by 1892, the ratio was almost one-to-one, wire nails to cut nails. Era: 1850 and after for brads and small nails; after 1880, for all uses.

a little practice. Find a piece of case furniture like a desk or a dresser that dates from the mid-Victorian period or earlier. Open a drawer, and slide your fingers across the underside of its bottom. If it was hand-planed, you'll feel a slight hill-and-valley texture. The waves of most hand-planed surfaces will vary less in amplitude, but the variations are still perceptible. A flashlight held at an acute angle to the grain of a board may also make the tool marks more visible.

Nowhere is the evidence of the handmade more obvious than in the moldings. Strips of wood used for finish or decorative purposes that have regular channels or projections are, by definition, moldings. At their simplest, moldings are transitions from one surface or material to another. A baseboard molding seems to join the floor to the wall, the cornice to link the wall to the ceiling. Casing or architrave moldings surround the windows and doors, and a chair rail is the molding that travels around the perimeter of the room at chair-back height to protect the plaster.

In the handmade age, moldings, as well as flat boards, were made with hand planes. The wood-molding plane was pushed along the length of a piece of wood and the contours

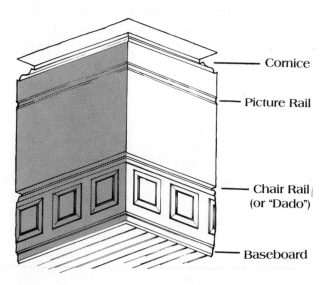

Cornice

Picture Rail

Chair Rail (or "Dado")

Baseboard

Plane Iron

As its name suggests, the molding plane was used to shape moldings. Its iron blade, sharpened to match the profile of the base of the wooden body, planed off shavings of the piece being shaped in a series of strokes. The heel of the right hand pushed from the rear, the left hand guided from the top.

of its iron blade cut the curves of the molding. In the case of simple moldings with shallow profiles, relatively few passes were required to shape the molding, as thin shavings of wood were removed with each stroke. With deep, complicated moldings, more time and effort was required.

To the uninitiated, moldings may seem so integral to their positions as to be inseparable from them. In fact, distinguishing different moldings is a valuable dating aid. The first step in doing so is recognizing that the cornice or the baseboard identifies a molding's *position;* the second, even more important, step is recognizing its shape or *profile.*

The curves and shapes of the molding can signify a good deal about the age, origin, and character of a handmade house. The moldings were to the finish work in the preindustrial age what the timber frame was to the rough carpentry, a labor-intensive process requiring the shaping of a raw material into usable form (a single doorway required shaping fifteen or more separate molding pieces). But the moldings also offered the builder in an age of rough-hewn wood the opportunity to create soft lines and shapes. It was an exercise in decoration, one that was rare in utilitarian structures.

READING MOLDINGS

To the trained eye, original moldings speak a clear and chronological language. There are several easy distinctions that even the novice can learn to make.

Greek versus Roman Moldings: One distinction is based on the Roman Rule: Roman moldings (and therefore Georgian and eighteenth-century American) are composed of portions of a circle. This distinguishes them from the later American Greek moldings that used portions of the ellipse for their curves. Though it is something of simplification, a molding profile with a distinguishably circular arc is probably eighteenth century; moldings of an elliptical shape are nineteenth century.

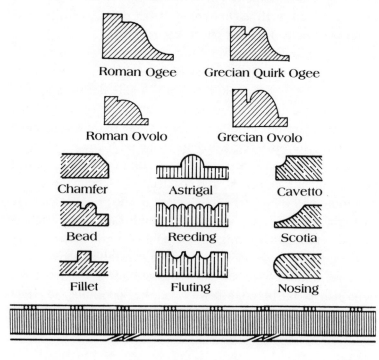

Roman Ogee	Grecian Quirk Ogee
Roman Ovolo	Grecian Ovolo

Chamfer	Astrigal	Cavetto
Bead	Reeding	Scotia
Fillet	Fluting	Nosing

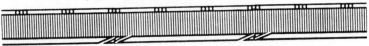

Molding Size and Relief: Eighteenth-century moldings are also flatter, broader, and lower than later ones. By the nineteenth century, the moldings are lighter but with greater relief.

Other Clues: In examining moldings, don't miss any other messages they have to offer. Try to detect any interruptions. Look for fixes or variations in shape. Disparities in the architrave, chair rail, cornice, baseboard, or other moldings can signify change. If the windows on one end of the room have moldings with a quite different profile from those at the other, there's a reason.

Follow each of the moldings around the room and around the house. Note and try to understand any breaks: Was a new door installed or one covered up? Perhaps a window was changed. Note the joints made at the junction of door architraves and baseboards: Are they the same everywhere?

You may not be able to tell when the changes were made, but knowing they occurred may spur other discoveries. If a cornice molding simply terminates in a corner rather than making the turn and continuing along its surface, that suggests the wall without the cornice was added.

Most moldings are now made of wood, but plaster moldings were common in nineteenth-century homes. Today, most moldings have little profile—that is, their thickness is uniform or varies only at one edge. In early homes, the relief was much greater and involved either the painstaking cutting and fitting of several pieces of molding or of a single, elaborately planed piece.

The molding plane, in fact, is a fitting symbol of how different that age was. Nothing was available off the shelf, yet so much of the workmanship bespoke not only a great deal of time invested, but also a concern for shape and quality. Appreciating a handmade house involves recognizing and understanding the role of handmade parts in its construction and decoration. To the carpenter/joiner before 1830, the choices to be made concerned what to make, not what to buy.

THE CHALLENGE OF CLIMATE

The prevailing building practices and available materials are always determining factors in house design—it's true today, just as it was at the time of the Roman Empire, and even during the reign of King Tut. But other influences are significant, too.

In the original thirteen colonies, the widely varying effects of climate were forces that had to be confronted. In North America, the Western European emigrants found a climate that was much less temperate than England's or Holland's. In New England, annual temperature swings routinely went from zero to 100 degrees Fahrenheit; in England, the usual range was more like 32 to 75.

In practical terms, the colder New England climate required design adjustments. To shed the snow, the roofs became steeper. The thatch that had sufficed in the Old World deteriorated in the New World and was shortly replaced by wooden shingling. The open-wall design, with its geometric patterns of structural timbers visible between areas of plaster or mud, which served the English at home simply crumbled in the face of a North American winter.

Inside the houses of the New World, other adjustments were necessary. The chimney became the focus of the design, with a center stack for as many as six fireplaces and accompanying flues creating an enormous, boxy masonry structure at the core of the house. In cold weather, this mass of stone or brick served to hold the heat from the fires and helped heat the house.

The situation was somewhat different in the southern colonies. Since the fireplace was the focus of food preparation all year round, it was the midsummer temperatures in Virginia that presented a problem. The solution that evolved also concerned chimney placement: in Colonial Virginia, chimneys were located in the end walls, often with their stacks constructed to stand away from the house itself, allowing the heat to dissipate outside rather than overheating the interior. Another solution was the summer kitchen—a complete, second kitchen was built either at the far extreme of the house or in another building altogether.

Building materials presented other problems. The earliest American houses were made entirely of wood, including the foundations. As a result, the lowest wooden members rotted away within a few years (which may account for the fact that there are no surviving examples of American architecture from before 1630, except for a handful of Spanish structures which were not constructed primarily of wood). The need for a foundation was a new problem for people coming from a world where the land had been deforested for generations so the standard building material was stone or brick. The frozen ground in the winter and resultant frost heaves in America also presented new problems. The solution was to dig a cellar beneath the house, a departure from European Continental building traditions.

From the first, American houses were indebted to the familiar, European buildings. Yet the New World demanded adjustments, both to the extremes of temperature and to the demands of an agricultural lifestyle on a heavily forested continent. The result was a fresh and distinct array of practical dwellings. Some of those houses benefited from a willingness to adopt the old ways to new circumstances, and a little good luck in the intervening centuries. Today, we can admire those enduring examples.

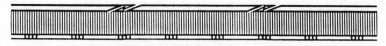

DOORS

Batten Doors: The earliest doors were batten doors, which were made of vertical boards, usually with tongues and grooves at their edges, that were clench nailed to other boards, the battens, which ran perpendicular to them. On exterior doors, the vertical boards face out and the entire interior of the door is lined with the horizontal batten boards. On interior doors, the battens were often limited to two or three individual boards. Batten doors usually had strap hinges (see page 81). Era: until ca. 1800 in main interior rooms; until well into the nineteenth century in rooms of secondary importance; until present day in barns and other outbuildings.

Rail-and-Stile Doors: Batten doors were simple, and the earliest urge for more decorative doors produced doors with moldings applied to their surfaces. The border moldings (the verticals are called "stiles," the horizontals, "rails") eventually became part of the structure of the door, with panels inset into them.

Later, rail-and-stile or "panel" doors evolved. These doors, held together by mortise-and-tenon joints, began to come into general use in the early eighteenth century. Era: After 1700.

The variations in paneled doors speak volumes, however, when it comes to distinguishing between Georgian, Adamesque, and Greek Revival houses. (See Reading Moldings, page 58.)

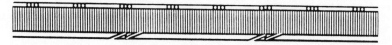

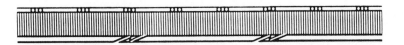

One dating trick for distinguishing early houses is to examine the door jambs (the vertical side of the doorway). The protrusion from the jamb that limits the swing of the door as it closes is called the "stop." If the stop consists of a separate piece of wood that has been applied to the jamb, the doorway dates from 1850 or later. In general, if the stop was cut into a solid jamb, it is earlier.

Though variations are common, as a rule eighteenth- and early nineteenth-century doors have six panels (four-panel doors are found as well, however, though more often in less important or less public locations like bed chambers). The nineteenth-century door typically has four panels, but the panels aren't necessarily rectangular in shape: they might have pointed Gothic arches or arched upper panels. In the twentieth century, all bets are off. Doors of all sorts were made from the earliest years of the century, including cross panels, vertical panels, combinations, with one to even eight panels, or none at all, as with the now common veneer door.

Don't kid yourself about the age of a door, however. Most modern doors could scarcely be mistaken for old ones upon careful inspection.

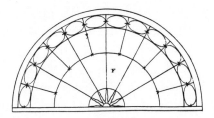

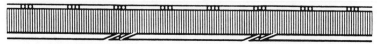

FIREPLACES AND CHIMNEYS

To examine your chimneys, start downstairs at the base. If you find masonry fireplace/chimney bases in the cellar but no indications upstairs of fireplaces or stovepipe intakes, it is possible they've been removed. On the other hand, they might simply have been covered over with plaster; the hearth might have been removed.

Look in the attic, too, at the point at which the chimney leaves the roof. Do all the roofing members appear to be of the same vintage, or are some of a different dimension or color? When a larger, earlier chimney has been replaced by a later, smaller stack, the new chimney has to be framed in with new wood.

Coal did not come into common use for fuel until the nineteenth century in the United States, though some East Coast cities had earlier burned imported British coal. The advent of coal meant a redesign of the firebox, making it narrower and smaller (a smaller amount of coal burns longer and more efficiently than wood). Oil heat didn't come into common use until after World War I.

If your house had coal grates (though the iron-faced fireboxes with relatively small pockets within them for coal are probably gone), then your fireplaces will be less than a foot deep. Coal burning became commonplace after 1825 in this country; if you suspect your house is older, you may well find that the coal fireplace you see was built within a larger, older one to take advantage of what was then the new

When the Obadiah Smith house was built ca. 1720, meals were prepared in this eight-foot-wide fireplace (above), with a range of iron utensils like those assembled on its hearth. By the time the Smithtown (New York) Historical Society acquired the house, however, centuries of changes had been introduced, including an entirely new firebox built within the original one (see below). *Credit: Smithtown Historical Society*

technology. (Note in the cellar whether there is any sign of a coal bin. The indications may be as obvious as a residue of coal in a corner somewhere or signs that a portion near a basement window was once partitioned off.)

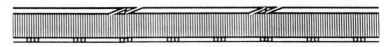

The fireplace mantel itself can also be a dating key. Houses in the eighteenth century had paneled walls around the fireplaces, while the Adamesque era saw delicate pilastered and decorated mantels come into vogue. Greek Revival mantels tend to have bold columns or pilasters with a full entablature. Arched mantels were very much the vogue from the 1850s to the 1870s, with marble ones, found in wealthier homes, often imported from Great Britain, France, or Italy. In fact, there was a considerable business of selling *faux* marble—that is, mantels made of slate but painted to resemble marble ("marbleized"). Later Victorian styles had elaborate galleried overmantels, but the Colonial Revival brought back both paneled and Adamesque styles. Craftsman houses often used rough brick and tiles, while catalogue houses usually had a combination of styles or mirrored wood mantels.

Georgian Paneled Wall, ca. 1775

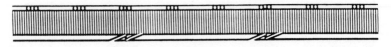

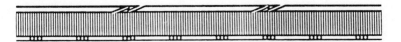

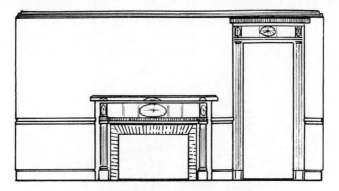

Federal Wall with Mantel, ca. 1800

Original wall coverings and fireplace mantels differed from one building style to the next. In the Georgian house (facing page), the panelling and mantel were integrated, and reached from floor to ceiling. In the Federal era, the wall was divided horizontally at the chair rail, and the mantel became a distinctly separate—and elegant—design element (above). By the Greek Revival period, the mantel was more stolid, its graceful pilasters blocky and the applied decorations of the Federal style abandoned. It stood virtually alone on the wall (below). Often, the Greek mantel was merely decorative—there was no traditional fireplace within, but a stove was plugged into its chimney.

Greek Revival Wall with Mantel, ca. 1840

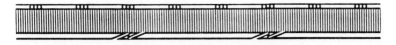

DUTCH COLONIAL:

1625–1820

This ca. 1900 drawing romanticizes a simple farmhouse, but nevertheless the shape of an early Dutch house is to be seen. Note the flared eaves (characteristic especially of the Hudson River valley) and the stone first-floor walls. The dormers are likely to have been a later addition.

Origins: The Dutch were known as the best brick masons in Europe, so it's hardly surprising that numerous Dutch houses in America were constructed of brick or stone. (Eighteenth-century Dutch brick is distinguished from its English counterpart by its size. Most early Dutch brick is longer and wider (about 9 inches by 4 1/2 inches), though later it came to be similar to the 8 inches by 4 inches English brick. However, Dutch brick remained thinner, 1 1/2 inches rather than 2 1/2 inches.)

Shape: The gambrel roof is not peculiarly Dutch, though during the Colonial Revival in the twentieth century the gambrel roof came to be a key attribute of a "Dutch Colonial" home (see page 140); in Colonial America, gambrel roofs were used by the English, Dutch, and other nationalities.

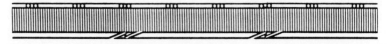

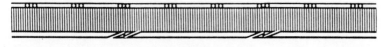

Typical early Dutch houses are one and a half stories tall with rooms on the second floor in the very steep gable or gambrel roof. The roof frequently flares beyond the front and rear of the house, providing a deep overhang.

Details: The timber frame of a Dutch style house resembles that of an English style house, but there are significant differences. A key one is the basic configuration of the bent: the Dutch style house is H-shaped, with an "anchor beam" forming the horizontal portion of the "H." (In an English timber frame, the girt—the equivalent of the anchor beam—sits atop the posts rather than only a portion of the way up their length). Dutch framing is most easily seen in Dutch barns.

Interior: Another difference in the Dutch framing system is that there were more bents, usually one every four feet or so (rather than, as in English framing, one between each bay or at about 16-foot intervals). In the Dutch style, beams line the ceilings of the first floor room (in English houses, the ceilings were plastered). These Dutch beams were characteristically large and hand-planed to a smooth surface, often with a molded curve cut onto their corners.

Doorway: The original front door of a Dutch house also distinguishes the structure. The classic Dutch door is divided horizontally, so the top and bottom halves operate independently.

Location: The Dutch dominated the Hudson Valley, New York, and portions of New Jersey and Pennsylvania.

STYLE
NOTES

ENGLISH
MEDIEVAL:

1603–1800

First published in 1904, this drawing of a medieval style
New England house suggests as much about the spirit of
the twentieth-century Colonial Revival as it does about the
seventieth-century house. In fact, life was more harsh than
picturesque when this house was built. A large dwelling for
its time, the two-story, five-bay house also has a shed addition at the rear. There's a massive center chimney, but the
plan is still but one room deep.

Origins: Early American houses in the English colonies were an amalgam of medieval English
styles using material and design compromises ne-
cessitated by the harsh North American climate.

Shape: Steeply pitched gable roofs are the
rule in English style houses. (It was what the English
knew: thatched roofs had to be steep to shed water.)
Many seventeenth-century houses were of the hall-
and-parlor variety, with just two rooms on the
ground floor—a "hall" for cooking, eating, and
working, and a "parlor" for use as a master bedroom.
After 1700, a separate kitchen to the rear was often

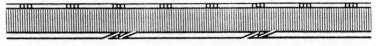

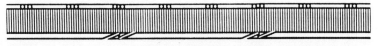

incorporated under the main roof of the house. Upstairs was an atticlike bedroom space.

Details: The Cape Cod house is representative of the early American house in the North. It is a one-story design, though a tall attic provided sleeping and storage accommodations; southern variations were also one room deep, and were more likely to have some decorative aspects in their brickwork. In some instances, the kitchen was in a shed addition to the rear, resulting in the characteristic shape known as a "saltbox" in the North (in the South, it's called a "cat's slide").

Doorways and windows: Batten doors were the rule until the early eighteenth century when panel doors appeared (see page 62). Until about 1725, the windows were small casements with diamond-shaped panes of glass called "quarrels." In the eighteenth century, the more familiar sash windows appeared with multiple small lights. By the second quarter of the eighteenth century, the pattern of the openings was more likely to be regular than utilitarian, as even modest vernacular dwellings typically had symmetrical façades.

Location: In the North, center chimneys and wood-frame construction were typical. In the South, it was end-wall chimneys and, at least to judge by surviving examples, brick structures. Adjustments made in Puritan New England were different from those made in plantation Virginia, but all simple early dwellings were boxy, plain houses.

SPANISH COLONIAL:

1565–1801

The Spanish Colonial differed greatly from Spanish Florida to the Southwest to California, but this rendering suggests some typical elements. Note the stucco walls; the low-pitched tile roof; and the multiple exterior doors (the interior rooms were not always connected from within).

Origins: The Spanish colonies stretched from Florida to California. The most impressive buildings that remain from the first Spanish settlements are ecclesiastical and governmental buildings, in particular missions and fortifications. These buildings were built by the powerful and wealthy Catholic Church or the Spanish Colonial government. Unlike English and Dutch Colonial buildings, Spanish Colonial structures were in keeping with the Spanish style on the European Continent and featured Baroque decorations.

Details: Spanish Colonial houses were much less elaborate than Spanish Colonial civic or religious structures. Built of a combination of timber and masonry, the houses were generally but one story

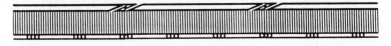

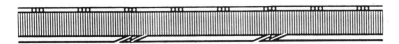

tall, and long and low with a covered porch. Many were built of adobe (*adobe* is Spanish for "brick"), which is made of sun-dried clay. In an adobe building, the bricks are stacked into wide walls, often several feet thick, which are then coated with a mixture of wet clay and gypsum. The roof consists of a structural layer of horizontal logs (called *vigas*) laid across the top of the walls and covered by a mass of branches, sticks, or reeds which, in turn, are covered with a thick coating of clay. In other regions, tile roofs were also common.

Location: Spanish style houses are found in the one-time Spanish colonies, especially Florida, New Mexico, and California. Despite the very fashionable and European quality of early Spanish Colonial architecture, it had little influence elsewhere in the United States.

THE EMERGENCE OF STYLE

Virtually all of the early settlers in North America were poor. They'd been among the lower classes in Europe, and they came to this land to improve their prospects. At first, the buildings they built were simple and practical, and style was a relatively minor consideration.

Their homes in America bore a greater resemblance to European houses of the Middle Ages than to the great Renaissance and Baroque structures being erected in Europe at that time. In the seventeenth century, in the era in which that architectural monument to royal excess, the colossal Versailles, was being constructed in Europe, the new arrivals on the North American coast were building little wooden houses in which the emphasis was not on style or elegance but on survival. In New England in particular there was even an attempt to *avoid* high style, along with the stratified society left behind in England. Small wooden dwellings were in keeping with the classless society the Puritans chose to establish. In the South, matters were only slightly different. Most of the buildings still had more in common with the England of Henry VIII than with that of King James I (for whom the 1607 settlement at Jamestown was named).

However, in Virginia, the plantation system, funded by venture capitalists in England or by individual proprietors on site, replicated some of the class structure of England. There were manor houses for the handful of wealthy arrivals, and their wealth was reflected in all aspects of their lives, including building materials. Brick was used more often, producing some quite elaborate houses.

The eighteenth century saw a significant stylistic advance, both in the North and South. In Chapter 1, we discussed timber-framing, the framing method that was used for virtually all houses in the handmade age. Many of the medieval-inspired early houses were three-bay timber-frame structures, but as civilization on these shores advanced, the houses grew. The three-bay house was joined by the five-bay configuration, in which the central door was flanked by two pairs of windows (an extra opening having been added in the extra bays at each end of the house).

The houses increased in depth as well as breadth. The new houses were two rooms deep, with two pairs of rooms, front-to-back, flanking the center entrance. This was the so-called "double-pile" configuration, as distinct from the smaller single-pile arrangement of the earlier floor plan. In New England, the single center chimney became two, one inside each of the interior walls that divided the front and back rooms. Upstairs space had usually been but attic bedroom(s), but the Georgian house had two full stories.

The larger house required two chimney stacks, and made the center stairs a prominent design element. Previously a

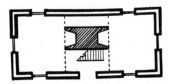

Hall-and-Parlor House

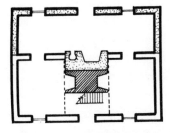

Single-Pile House with Shed Addition

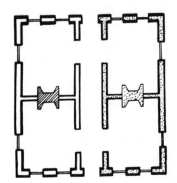

Double-Pile House

The development was logical: the simple two-room house
became one with three rooms (at first) and then four. It was
the second increase that also signaled the arrival of the
stylish Georgian house.

twisted and angular affair attached like a Siamese twin to the
center chimney, the stairway in the center-hall house was open
and airy, an opportunity to announce to the visitor that he or
she was in the presence of people of some means.

The double-pile configuration was characteristic of a new
eighteenth-century style, the Georgian, named after the En-

glish kings in power after 1714. Not all eighteenth-century houses are Georgian, for the seventeenth-century medieval style house continued to evolve. But the Georgian house in eighteenth-century America represented the first widespread attempt by American builders to construct houses of evident, self-conscious design. The simple, even crude unadorned structures were replaced, at least for the wealthy, by houses of conscious style and decoration. The improvement was more a matter of taste and economics than of technology. In fact, until the end of the century, the only significant changes in materials and techniques were the frequent use of plaster and paint, long used in Europe, but relatively rare in seventeenth-century America.

In the Georgian house, the front entry became a statement, with adornments of Classical orders of columns (or pilasters) with pediments above. The windows were almost invariably multilight double-hung windows. The cornice (the projecting portion of the roof) had molded shapes; the corners of the building had quoins or pilasters. The building material was often brick (especially in the southern United States; in New England, wood continued to be more common). Inside, the ceilings were taller and the rooms carefully proportioned and detailed.

The Georgian house was the dominant style for larger homes from about 1725 until the Revolution. It was succeeded by the Federal or "Adamesque" style, to a great degree a variation on the same theme. It, too, was based on English precedents, deriving one of its names from a pair of English brothers, Robert and James Adam, who developed a distinct decorative mode. Its more common name, Federal, comes from its emergence during the era in which the Federalist party was dominant. Whatever you call it, the style was a reaction.

After the Revolution, there was an emotional need to disassociate American culture from things British: "freedom" was the watchword in more than just politics. Yet the typical Adamesque house is closer to the Georgian than many of its designers would have liked to admit. From a distance, the

This handsome Georgian doorway (above, left) features a
semi-circular fan-light window and fluted pilasters flanking
a door with six raised panels. Dentils decorate the open pediment. In comparison, the Federal doorway (above, right)
has elongated, lighter decorations—despite its size, it's almost delicate, with its sun-rise fan sash. The Greek Revival
entrance (below, left) resumes the boldness of the Georgian,
and even enlarges the elements. The Victorian entrance
boasts two doors, but is much simpler: in the Victorian age,
other aspects of the house were more likely to be heavily
decorated than the doorway.

resemblance is particularly strong: both are double-pile structures, with pairs of rooms on either side. Both have center entrances and broad halls bisecting the house. Symmetry is the rule. But there are also significant differences.

The Federal style rejected what were regarded as the decorative excesses of the Georgian. There were smaller or no pilasters on either side of the entrance (though there was a characteristic fan sash, usually elliptical in shape, over the door, and a pair of sidelights on either side). While quoins on the corners of the house became rare, they weren't unheard of. To confuse matters, there was occasionally a columned portico.

Other differences are apparent on closer examination. Robert Adam had spent time studying the ancient monuments in Italy, having visited the recently discovered remains of ancient civilizations at Pompeii and Herculaneum. As a result, he brought to English architecture a firsthand familiarity with Classical antiquity. Previously, the ancients had been seen through the Renaissance eyes of Italian scholars and builders, in particular, Andrea Palladio, whose buildings and books were key sources for Georgian architects.

The Adams' contribution to architecture here and in Great Britain was greater in the details than in the shapes. Their interiors were refined, rich with plaster details. Swags and garlands were favored design elements on exterior cornices and architraves, as were urns and other geometric designs. It is these decorations that set the Adamesque style apart from the Georgian: rather than relying on curved moldings or architectural echoes of columns or other Classical elements, the brothers Adam applied their urns and swags with abandon.

In this country, the Adamesque/Federal style was first associated with the great Boston architect Charles Bulfinch, who designed numerous church and public buildings, including the Massachusetts State House, as well as residences. He has been credited by many with introducing the Adamesque style, but it was the writer/carpenter Asher Benjamin who made it widely available beyond the wealthy urban centers.

Benjamin was a working carpenter in central New Eng-

This 1814 house in Chatham Center, New York, may require some paint and other attention, but it still speaks with
the eloquence of the brothers Adam. The fan-carved architrave, the cornice details, the elliptical attic openings, and
the Palladian window identify it as a Federal style dwelling—and the work of a gifted carpenter/builder.

land who, by 1803, when he moved to Boston, had built widely
in Connecticut, Massachusetts, and Vermont. Once in the big
city, he found himself keeping up with the latest trends and
working in the Adamesque manner of Bulfinch. In his pattern
book, *The American Builder's Companion* of 1806, he described
an ever more Federal/Bulfinch/Benjamin Adamesque style.
(Benjamin's first book, *The Country Builder's Assistant*, published in 1797, which was the earliest American architectural
work, was less Adamesque.)

The American Builder's Companion reached a wide reader-
ship. This and other of Benjamin's books were tailored to the
predominantly wooden American house. The style described
was English, yet it was transformed: it was thinner, more at-
tenuated, and more in tune with the materials being used
(namely wooden boards rather than blocks of stone). In fact,

Benjamin's slendering of proportion, though subtle, is one of the key distinguishing characteristics of Adamesque buildings.

The American handmade house is one built between the European settlement on these shores and the advent of the machinery that we will discuss at length in the chapter that follows. It began as a response to the simple and immediate need for shelter, and, at first, the handmade house closely re-

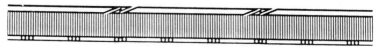

HARDWARE

The hardware elements on doors are among the best clues to the age of a house—that is, if they haven't been replaced by some overzealous renovator. Remember, if the latch or lock is original, the surface beneath will not have been painted. If it has been, then the latch or lock was added later. During any renovation work that involves scraping a door, be alert for signs of a latch or locking mechanisms, even if the door was painted. You may find signs of repairs, such as patches of nail or screw holes, or the outline of an earlier lock or latch. Paint-scraping will often disclose the form and size of an earlier latch or lock.

Most early hardware was wrought iron, the material with which the blacksmith works. To shape it, the material is successively heated and hammered. Its finish is the result of repeated firings, which cause a black oxide scale to form on the iron's surface. It is an identifiably handmade product: it is not perfectly symmetrical, its thickness varies from one

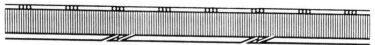

sembled the houses known to the settlers back in Europe.

As prospects improved in the eighteenth century, so did the houses. Gradually, larger, grander structures appeared, and the English Georgian took its place just up the street from the simpler, medieval-inspired homes, like the Cape Cod and the saltbox, that had evolved to suit the climate in the New World. After the Revolution, the Adamesque or Federal style satisfied the changed tastes and emotional needs of a newly independent land.

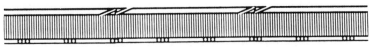

section to another, and its surface bears the imprint of numerous hammer strokes.

Brass was used for hinges (though largely on fancy furniture) and for other hardware in the eighteenth century. In the second half of the nineteenth century, it became widely popular, especially in the form of brass-plated hardware.

Brass, like iron, is malleable, but in contrast to iron it can even be worked cold. Much Victorian hardware was made by stamping or hammering cold brass into molds. It was also used for knobs, though after 1840 the manufacture of brass knobs was rare. Brass, when polished, has a yellowish tinge.

Strap Hinges: While virtually all hardware used in this country until after about 1825 was made in Great Britain, there is an important exception to this "import rule": blacksmiths here often made the large, heavy strap hinges.

A strap hinge looks like a strap. Though strap hinges can be as short as 12 inches, they are more often 2 feet or longer. They are attached horizontally with rivets or nails. One end of the strap hinge ex-

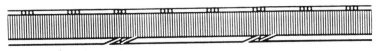

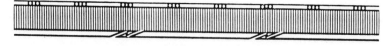

tends slightly beyond the edge of the door and is curved back upon itself to form a vertical, cylindrical cavity (an "eye"). The door with the hinges already affixed is lowered onto "pintels"—L-shaped iron pegs. The pointed base of the L is driven like a nail into the door jamb, while the eye of the strap hinge is lowered onto the upright portion of the L.

Used in America from the seventeenth century on, the strap hinge faded in popularity by the turn of the eighteenth century, though it continued to be used on barns and outbuildings and, occasionally, on other exterior doors throughout most of the nineteenth century. Era: until ca. 1825 for interiors, ca. 1875 for exteriors and outbuildings.

H and HL Hinges: These are among the easiest objects in the world to identify: they look exactly like their names suggest. Screws as well as nails were used to attach the handwrought hinges. Like strap hinges, they were made of wrought iron, but were generally of English manufacture. Nailed or screwed (in fancier houses), these hinges went out of fashion by about 1810 or 1820, earlier in many areas. Era: until ca. 1815.

Cast Butt Hinges: Since these hinges were made by casting rather than by being wrought by a blacksmith, they were less labor intensive and cheaper. As their name suggests, they also fit into

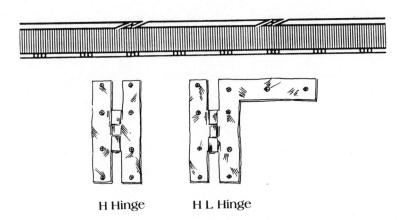

H Hinge   H L Hinge

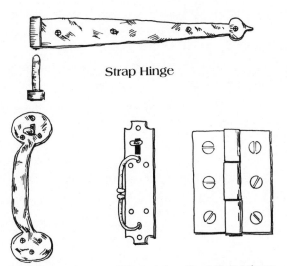

Strap Hinge

Suffolk Latch   Norfolk Latch   Cast Butt Hinge

the butt joint where the door and its jamb met, so they were less visible. They were usually attached with screws.

Some wrought butt hinges were made earlier, but cast butt hinges were patented in England in

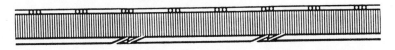

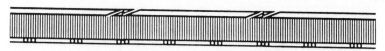

1775. They were common here by 1800. The early ones had fixed pins, but after about 1830 or 1840 loose butts came into use. These hinges were intended to be painted. After 1850, stamped butt hinges became common. Era for fixed-pin butts: 1775 to ca. 1830. Era for loose butts: 1860 to 1900.

Suffolk Latches: Suffolk latches originally came from Suffolk, England, but the name became a generic term for all latches with no back plate.

The Suffolk latch is largely an eighteenth-century phenomenon. Most Suffolk latches were made in England and were fixtures on Georgian and early Adamesque houses. However, the Arts and Crafts movement enthusiastically adopted the Suffolk latch, so many were made around the beginning of the twentieth century for Craftsman and other homes. While most of the revival examples were machine-made, the originals were wrought by blacksmiths. Era: late seventeenth century to ca. 1825; later revivals.

Norfolk Latches: Unlike the Suffolk latch, the Norfolk latch has a full back plate. It replaced the Suffolk latch in general use after about 1820 and was usual on Greek Revival houses. Though early versions were handwrought in England, the large majority in this country were made by machinery. Many had cast- or wrought iron handles, with stamped back plates and decorations cut onto their tops and bottoms. Era: 1800 to 1850.

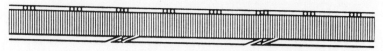

GEORGIAN:

1720–1800

Pictured in this nineteenth-century woodcut is a prototypical Georgian house in Germantown, Pennsylvania. It is a grand house, complete with a projecting pavilion at center front and pedimented dormers on the roof. The material is stone, the windows 12/12s, the design double-pile with two massive chimneys.

Origin: The Georgian house was based on Italian Renaissance sources (principally Andrea Palladio's *The Four Books of Architecture*, as translated by English tastes of the day).

Shape: Formality and symmetry are essential concepts to keep in mind for identifying the Georgian house. The Georgian façade is balanced, two stories tall, and topped with a gable or hip roof and a pair (or two pairs) of chimneys. On the first story, an elaborate doorway at the center is flanked by evenly spaced pairs of windows on either side. Above are five windows aligned with the openings below. The roofs are steep, commonly with dormers. Narrow clapboard or masonry construction is usual.

Details: Classical elements are the rule, and the more the better. Pilasters or quoins adorn the

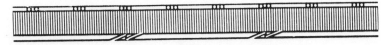

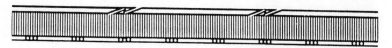

corners, and the cornice is decorated, often with toothlike dentils.

Doorway: In America, it is the elaborate center doorway that is to be regarded as the hallmark of the Georgian style (several of the carpenter books of the era went so far as to refer to the entrance as the "frontispiece"). The door surround is usually pedimented, often with columns and other Classical motifs. In fancy homes, the door and the window above are emphasized by a projecting, two-story pavilion. An arched window over the doorway is common, and the door itself is paneled.

Windows: With the Georgian house, the sliding sash window arrived, always with many panes of glass. Commonly, 12/12s in the North, 9/9s in the South. Other configurations are also found (including 9/6s and 12/8s), but 6/6s are likely to indicate a post-Revolutionary War house (or an Adamesque-style building). The muntins are quite thick, half an inch or more wide, and the upper sash is fixed in place.

The Palladian or Venetian window is also common, usually after 1750. The Palladian window is to be found on the second story, aligned with the entryway below.

Interior: Central halls flanked by pairs of rooms on each side are the rule. Walls are paneled floor to ceiling or are plastered with a crown molding and finished with wainscotting.

Location: Georgian houses were common in East Coast trading towns, in some inland villages, and on plantations.

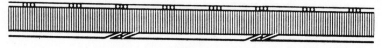

FEDERAL

1780–1820

This drawing from the Historic American Buildings Survey is of a house in Savannah, Georgia. Built in 1815, the Davenport house features the classic elliptical fan sash over the front door, but in general has fewer and simpler decorations than the earlier Georgian. *Credit: HABS*

Origin: The Federal house was partly a reaction to Great Britain, a simplifying of the English Georgian house. But it was also an adaptation of the work of Robert and James Adam and of their book *The Works in Architecture* and the numerous borrowings of their ideas in Asher Benjamin's and other pattern books (thus the style's alternate name, Adamesque). It was in the Adamesque house that the French innovation, the built-in closet, appeared for the first time in some of America's fancier bedrooms.

Shape: The Federal house is two or three stories tall, and most often hip-roofed. The square or rectangular shape of the house and the arrangement of its windows and doors closely resemble those of the Georgian house, but the roof is flatter.

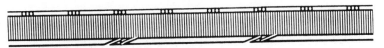

Details: Exteriors are clapboard or brick, though suspiciously lacking the decorative Classical details common to Georgian houses. There are no quoins and fewer, thinner moldings. Rather than relying on Classical architectural elements, the Federal house depends upon careful proportions and the materials themselves to complete the picture. Though some Adamesque houses will have swags or garlands or urns applied to their cornices or architraves, the style is characteristically plain and simple.

Doorway: One of the hallmarks of a Federal house is the elliptical fan sash over the doorway, usually with flanking sidelights. In many examples, a portico with full Classical orders may stand before the doorway.

Windows: The rule is 6/6 sash windows. The windows tend to be narrower in the Adamesque than in the Georgian house, and the muntins thinner.

Interior: If the exterior is all about letting quality materials and good breeding speak for itself, then the Adamesque interior is positively showy, though in an elegant way, with its decorated mantels, window frames, cornices, and ceilings. Wood moldings and applied plaster ornamentation are usual: delicate curves blended with rosettes and swags and garlands, compliments of the brothers Adam.

Location: Found along the Eastern Seaboard in the original colonies, usually in wealthier port cities and towns as homes for the merchants, shipbuilders, and bankers. In the South, the roofs tended to be taller and, as usual, the material brick.

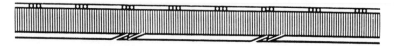

4.

THE
VICTORIAN
HOUSE

1830–1900

The repeated, rhythmic hisses and booms and bangs of the machine produce identical objects. Each machine-made nail or clapboard or pipe is supposed to be the same as the one before and the one after. If it isn't, it is not salable.

An object shaped by the human hand is unique. It may have been well or badly made, but, by definition, it bears the imprint of its maker.

Which is "better"? That may seem a silly question, but it's one that we must ask ourselves as we look at old buildings. Half the answer is that something made well by a machine is likely to be "better" than a similar object made by a poor workman. But the second half of the answer is a good deal more complicated.

Engineering studies tell us that a beam made of several pieces of lumber laminated together is much stronger than a beam of the same size made of a single timber. You may not need an engineer to tell you that, if you live with bowed old timbers riddled with checks. In the parlance of the woodsman, they're the cracks that occur at the heart, or pith, of the tree. Is the new, machine-fabricated laminated beam better?

What if the solid timber was put in place before 1800? And what if its surface is textured, bearing witness to the elbow grease invested by its shaper using a hand plane to smooth it? Perhaps it even has a shape on its edge, a chamfered or beaded corner? Perhaps it's the original Venetian red or Prussian blue, its colors a deep hue that comes only with time and wood smoke and the life of a house. Does that make the old timber better? It's harder to keep clean than a smooth, less porous modern surface. Perhaps our old beam also has signs of insect infestation on one end, and nail holes along its length from a hundred years or more spent with plaster lath nailed to it.

One can talk endlessly about the terrible toll exacted upon the caliber of workmanship by machines and factory-made parts. It is largely true that machines and machine-made goods have combined to vanquish craftsmen of all sorts, and with them the satisfaction that goes with crafting something well. On the other hand, many machines have made possible more decorative adornments for more people. In the handmade age, architectural details were primarily for the privileged.

It took time to hand shape the moldings, pilasters, wooden quoins, and other adornments for a Georgian or Adamesque house, while the Greek Revival and American Gothic buildings that followed were often decorated with architectural elements that were machine-made, in some instances in factories, and thus were purchased ready-to-install. Industrial progress, some argue persuasively, made it possible for more people to live not only more stylishly but more comfortably, for the advances brought mass-produced stoves, glass, plumbing fixtures, and other goods.

In between those early years of industrialism and the twentieth century was the age of Victoria, during which Americans seemed to crave variety more than anything else.

With the machinery to manufacture and the means to deliver the goods, all that was required was for the consumers to develop a taste for the new and different. To judge from the unprecedented variety of styles and decorations to be found in and on American Victorian houses, our ancestors took full advantage of the stylistic and material choices available to them.

The changes that took place during the first half of the nineteenth century were as great as in any period of American history. They were many and rapid, but a few of them stand out. In particular, there is the advent, in the 1830s, of the railroad (by 1840 there were 2,800 miles of railroad track; forty years later, there were 40,000). Steamboats and canals and locks get part of the credit, too, for linking American society to itself. (Though the first canal opened in the 1790s, it was in the 1820s that canal-building was at its peak.) Among other benefits, canals and steamboats made possible the shipment of the large iron members required for the construction of iron railroad bridges and aqueducts.

Canals and railroads opened up markets and made raw materials available not only at the source, but anywhere a canal barge or railroad train traveled. A rapidly growing population was waiting to be served. Between 1820 and 1860, the population tripled, from about ten million to about thirty-one million souls.

The Victorian age in American architecture was the greatest era of construction the world has ever seen. While not all buildings were of uniformly high quality, much imaginative and innovative work was done. The first full century of the industrial age produced such a staggering volume of houses that even today many, many American communities owe much of their character to the homes of that period.

During the nineteenth century, the millions of houses built benefited from a marriage of the handmade tradition and the explosive growth of manufacturing. In fact, if the preceding era is best characterized by the transparent elegance of the handmade, then the Victorian age is to be identified with its confusing profusion of machine-made materials.

FROM THE GREEK TO THE GOTHIC

Understanding the Victorian house requires some knowledge of the machinery that made its decorations possible and affordable. Equally important is a bit of archaeological cum architectural history.

Just as the brothers Adam found inspiration in ancient (Roman) ruins, the styles that succeeded the Federal/Adamesque were based upon discoveries about ancient architecture. In 1763, the German archaeologist Johann Winckelmann published his masterwork, *History of Ancient Art,* making a bold, new case for Greek art and architecture. Until Winckelmann's time, Greek culture hadn't been distinguished from Roman, but Winckelmann argued convincingly that Greek architecture was, in fact, the source of all subsequent architectural forms.

With Winckelmann's scholarship lighting the way, the Greek Revival was suddenly possible. The style was never widely popular in Europe, but in the United States it seemed a natural fit. The first Greek Revival building in this country is thought to have been the Bank of Pennsylvania (1799), but it was in the late 1820s that the same Asher Benjamin whose books had helped deliver the Adamesque style to the hinterlands helped popularize the Greek style.

It was Benjamin's fifth, 1826 edition of *The American Builder's Companion* that incorporated the Greek orders. Another writer of builder's books, Minard Lefever, in his *The Modern Builder's Guide* (1833) provided more Grecian-inspired designs and practical guidance. Carpenters who had no more chance of locating Greece on a map than of finding Pluto in the heavens (it hadn't been discovered yet) managed to transform trees into shapely, wooden, *Greek* structures.

The Greek Revival style was the first architectural style in which Americans truly invested their individuality. (As we have seen, the Georgian and the Adamesque styles were highly derivative of English sources.) Its longevity speaks for the comfortable fit it seems to have had for generations of Americans. Dating a Greek Revival house is difficult to do by style alone, as some buildings as early as the turn of the nineteenth century have Greek elements, though the style is usually assigned the time span of 1820 to 1850. Yet even in the areas of its greatest and earliest popularity, the South and New England, Greek Revival homes were constructed well into the 1850s and 1860s; in California, Greek-style houses were still being built in the 1870s.

Perhaps it was sympathy for the Greeks themselves, who, in the 1820s, were fighting a war of independence. Maybe it was a young country's desire for a sense of history, of a connection with an ancient culture. Perhaps there was a need, conscious or unconscious, to adopt a style apart from that current in Britain in order to escape the tyranny of British taste. Whatever the reason, the Greek Revival was the dominant style in the early years of the Victorian era.

Yet it was by no means the only one. The Greek Revival was barely under way when a similar, historically based architectural movement, the Gothic Revival, appeared. As usual, the style had first emerged in eighteenth-century Britain. There it had appeared as a by-product once again of a new archaeological and scientific spirit. To their surprise, scholars had determined that there were distinct periods separating the centuries of Gothic buildings (the "Early English" flourished from 1200 to 1300; the "Decorated," from 1300 to 1350; and the "Perpendicular," from 1350 to 1550). In England, the findings led to much study of the plentiful medieval buildings and a taste for new architectural exercises in the style.

In the United States, the Gothic Revival was actually more a matter of technological change than historical research. The single most important advance in the shaping of wood was the advent of the circular saw (it was widely used in the 1830s, and identifying circular and other saw cuts are a key dating technique, as discussed in Chapter 1), but it was the steam-powered scroll saw that gave the Gothic Revival a peculiarly American twist.

To the uninitiated, the tool might resemble a sewing machine with a narrow reciprocating blade rather than a needle. As with the seam made by a sewing machine, the cuts made by a scroll saw are determined only by the operator's desires. Zigzags, curves, or complicated shapes were formed simply by adjusting the angle of the board as it approached the blade. The classic example of scroll-saw work is the "bargeboard" (also called "vergeboard") on the American Gothic house: the elaborately cut boards that face the projections of gable roofs.

Its vergeboard seemingly dripping with gingerbread, this striking drawing from Downing's *Cottage Residences* suggests some of the decorative possibilities of new power cutting tools and the Gothic mode.

The scroll saw made American Gothic different. A scroll saw blade is positioned perpendicular to the surface of the wood fed to it, and as a result, wood cut with it has two-dimensional curves, unlike the stone in medieval Gothic (and most English Gothic Revival) buildings, which was carved into three dimensions. The change in material (stone to wood) and technique (chiseling to scroll-sawing) produced a distinctly different decoration.

Today scroll-saw cut woodwork is often called "gingerbread." One of the key proponents of the Gothic style, Andrew Jackson Downing, disliked the name, however, objecting that to term the fanciful and decorative wooden ornaments "gingerbread" was to reduce them to "flimsy and meager decorations which have a pasteboard effect." Succeeding generations dismissed gingerbread and other Victorian age decorations as excessive or grotesque, but more recently there has been an emerging admiration for such work, and even a move to replicate it in new buildings.

Along with the circular saw and scroll saw came other wood-shaping power tools, including the machine planer. Machine planing arrived in 1828 with the Woodworth planer; another machine, the Daniels planer, was patented in 1834.

These machines saved incalculable man hours. An easy glide through a steam-powered planer took but a few seconds, while even a skilled workman required many minutes of work to accomplish the same task. The planer made possible the board-and-batten siding (in which the siding consists of wide vertical boards with narrow battens nailed over their joints) popular in the American Gothic style seen in and after the 1840s. By the 1850s, most boards were machine-planed. (Some of the early planers used circular blades, and, as a result, the marks left may resemble circular saw marks.)

Moldings, too, came to be machine made. An early machine had been patented in England before the turn of the century, but it wasn't until the 1840s that curved and shaped moldings were being made by machines in the United States. As with most advances, however, molding machines weren't immediately available everywhere. One early center of lumber processing was Troy, New York. There, machine-made moldings were available even before they were in New York City. The machine-processed goods gradually made their way, by canal and railway, to other areas. In communities not serviced by such modes of transportation, the technology arrived later.

The moldings made by machine molding planes are distinguishable from those made with hand planes if the plane marks haven't been sanded or scraped smooth. The rotating cutter of the power molding plane leaves marks at a 90-degree angle to the molding's length, while a hand plane, since its blade is set at an angle to the piece, leaves marks at an angle of about 45 degrees (see discussion of hand-planing, page 56).

MORE
MACHINE-MADE
GOODS

Throughout the Victorian age, there was a constant flow of new, machine-made products. Several such innovations are likely to be found in the houses that survive from the era.

Handmade Screws: After 1790, the wood screw came into widespread use, mostly with the increasing popularity of the cast butt hinge (see page 82). These early screws were made by hand. They had heads, and their threads were cut with a manual threading device. While various machines had been invented for steps in the screw-making process, none of these early screws tapered to a point. Also, the threads varied greatly because the tools used to cut the threads were made by hand. A pointless screw can be detected without removing it: the slots on the heads of early screws were also handmade, so they are often off center. Era: 1790 to ca. 1850.

Pointless Screw   Machine-Made Screw,
                                  After 1846

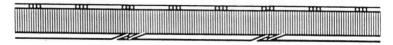

Machine-made Screws: Screws didn't

have points until 1846, when a machine was invented to make them. (U.S. Patent No. 4704, dated August 10th, 1846, to be exact). They were rapidly adopted after that date; their use saved a step in installation because a hole didn't have to be cut—by hand, of course—with an awl or other drilling tool. Era: after 1850.

Blake's Patent Latch: The perfect dating

clue is an object that is easy to identify and of a definite date, such as the Blake's Patent latch.

The Blake latch was patented in 1840. Made of cast- rather than wrought iron, the Blake's Patent latch is distinguishable from its ancestor, the Suffolk latch (see page 84), by the relative thickness of its iron; it is heavy and clumsy in comparison to the earlier latch. The Blake's Patent latch was mass-produced and sold through catalogues. Era: 1840 to 1920.

Rim Locks: After 1840, many house build-

ers installed iron or, less frequently, brass locks with knobs rather than latches. Because of the ease of installation, latches didn't disappear, but after that date devices with knobs gradually became the rule for most interior applications. Era: 1840 to 1925.

Rim locks were surface-mounted iron boxes. Although used in fancier houses throughout most of the eighteenth century, they dominated the domestic market from about 1840 until after the beginning of the twentieth century. They are distin-

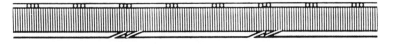

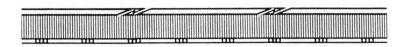

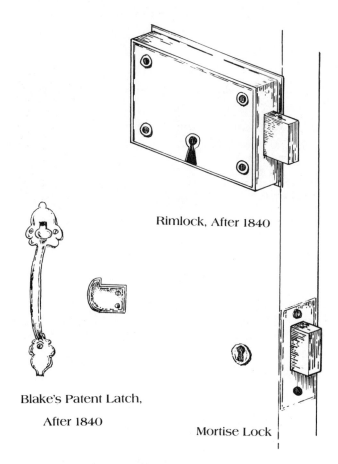

Rimlock, After 1840

Blake's Patent Latch,
After 1840

Mortise Lock

guished from most locks today by the fact they were mounted on the surface of the door (that is, the "rim"); most new locks are "mortise" locks—that is, they are mortised into the door itself. While the mortise lock was used as early as the late eighteenth century, it was little more than an occasional curiosity until after 1850.

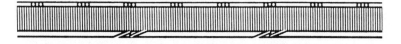

GREEK REVIVAL:

1820–1860

Pictured in this 1876 illustration is a Greek Revival house with characteristic temple front, flanked by a wing (probably for the kitchen). It's a proud house, with its columned portico, wide entablature, and pediment.

Origins: As a result of eighteenth-century archaeological discoveries, Classical Greece made its way to America in such books as *The Antiquities of Athens*. Architect Benjamin Latrobe used the Greek Revival style as early as 1799, but it wasn't until writer/carpenters like Asher Benjamin published pattern books that it reached the general population in the 1820s.

Shape: The most familiar Greek Revival house has the shape of a Classical temple, with the gable-end façade decorated like the Parthenon. The roof, in comparison to earlier Georgian (and later Victorian styles, especially Gothic Revival), has a relatively low slope. In the vernacular, however, the Greek style was translated in America into virtually all shapes. The traditional medieval box shape is

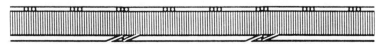

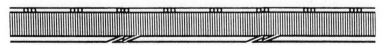

among the most common, though usually with the gable turned to face the street.

Room arrangements were more flexible than in earlier houses. Despite the strongly symmetrical aspect of the façade front, the inside of the house often wasn't symmetrical. One typical layout of a middle-class house consisted of a gable front, with the entrance to one side (misleadingly termed "side-hall Colonial" by some). Another common asymmetrical configuration featured a symmetrical façade with no entryway, but with an ell, set back from the front and to one side, that featured a porch with the entrance.

Details: The roof has a shallow slope, and its lower ends are usually connected to form a triangular pediment which is, in turn, supported by columns or pilasters. A wide band of trim is evident (a full entablature with bold cornice, frieze, and architrave) just beneath the roof, though as the style became increasingly vernacular, it also became simpler. There were fewer moldings, and more porches appeared. Dormers are rare. The most common color for Greek revival exteriors was white of various shades, though brick and stone examples were left unpainted.

In the preceding chapter, we discussed the handwrought nail, which had to be made by hand, required precious raw material, and took considerable time to produce (see page 52). The advent of its successor, the machine-made "cut" nail, had a significant impact upon house-building.

Between about 1790 and 1830, cutting machinery utterly

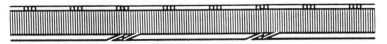

Doorways: Characteristic doorways have pilasters on the side and elaborate headpieces suggestive of their antecedents, the trabeated stone structure of the Greek temple. Often the doorway is set back a foot or more from the plane of the façade and is accompanied by a rectangular transom and sidelights. Porticos are also found on some examples. (See photograph, page 77.)

Windows: The windows tend to be 6/6s, although very late in the period 2/2s became common. They are usually boldly molded. In story-and-a-half examples, small "eyebrow" windows located just beneath the roof overhang in the frieze provide light for second-floor rooms. Shutters were common.

Interior: Inside, the Greek Revival house was almost spartan in comparison to the Federal house. The parlor often had a heavy cornice and decorations, but the rest of the house tended to have only simply molded architraves and plaster walls. Marbleized or grained doors and trim were common.

Location: In the North, the columns were often incorporated into the façade as pilasters; in the South, a full portico was more likely; both were accommodations to climate.

transformed the making of nails. The first nail-cutting machines were powered by human muscle power, but water and steam power were adopted shortly. As in the making of hand-wrought nails, the nail-cutting process again began with a prefabricated material, but, rather than a rod, the material was a plate of iron, usually about two inches wide, an eighth of

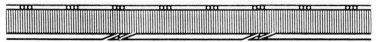

PLASTER
AND LATH

One valuable trick to learn is how to detect plaster.
It's a question of sound: when you knock on a wall
you know is plasterboard, the sound is different from
that produced when knocking on a surface that has
a real, so-called "wet plaster" surface. The drywall
is thinner and offers a hollow sound. The plastered
wall, with its lath and several layers of plaster, is
almost soundproof. The plasterboard echoes, the
plaster thuds.

If you detect a pattern of bumps the size of nail
heads (called "nail pops") or cracks or lines that echo
the 4-by-8-foot dimensions of a sheet of plasterboard
(namely joint or tape lines) your walls are probably
gypsum board. The only way to be certain about a
wall's materials is to take it apart and examine the
inner layers. In this way you may discover one
method of resurfacing plaster walls that has become
common practice in recent years. When the old
plaster cracks, the shortcut many contractors rec-
ommend is to apply a layer of drywall on top of the
old plaster.

Plaster cracks, nail holes from picture hangers,
and dangling pieces of moldings can be windows
into the construction past of your house. They offer
an opportunity to examine the structure of the wall
without doing substantial demolition. Removing
plug and switch covers from electrical boxes (cut off
the power first) will sometimes reveal the wall construction. Can you see layers of wallpaper? What

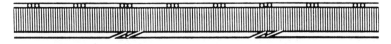

about paint? Is the wood lath visible beneath the plaster?

Another trick in examining plaster is to look at it after dark, using a powerful flashlight. Rake the light at an acute angle to the wall, and imperfections in the surface will be revealed. You may be able to detect repairs, or even ghosts of a long-removed chair rail or a one-time opening for a window or door in the wall.

Plaster is difficult to date, but the lath can be an invaluable key. Plaster requires support, and, like the armature of a clay sculpture, plaster lath prevents the plaster from crumbling and cracking. It isn't worth demolishing a perfectly good plaster wall to get a look at its supporting structure, but be on the lookout for exposed lath. Stairwells, closets, and attics may offer glimpses of lath on the hidden side of walls and the tops of ceilings.

Until about 1825, most lath was hand-split or "riven." Riven lath is, thus, a valuable dating tool indicating a preindustrial age house (riven lath is distinguishable by its uneven, hatchet-marked surface). Sometimes you'll find "accordion lath," in which a thin (typically, 3/8 inch thick) but wide (at least 12 inches) piece of sawn wood is split from alternate edges to form an accordionlike piece. After the advent of the circular saw, more regular pieces of lath came into use. These slats are rough-cut, but of uniform thickness and width, and remained dominant until after 1880.

After about 1900, a wire-mesh lath was introduced; after about 1920 both rock lath and plas-

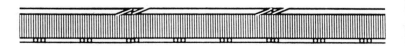

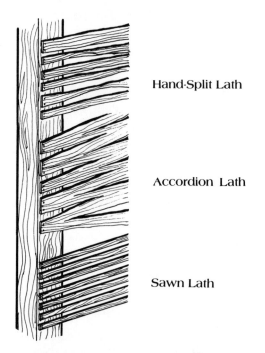

Hand-Split Lath

Accordion Lath

Sawn Lath

terboard came to be more frequently used (see Chapter 5 for discussion of plasterboard). As usual, however, the transition from wooden lath to its more modern alternatives didn't happen overnight. The metal lath, because of its greater resistance to fire, was first widely used in public buildings and apartment houses, while the sawn wood lath continued to be popular for domestic applications until well into the 1930s and even the 1940s.

If possible, examine the nails that attach the lath to the walls. Wire nails suggest that the strips of lath date from after about 1880.

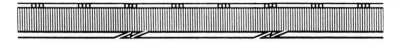

an inch thick, and several feet long (the plate varied in size depending upon the size of the nails to be made). This time a device with a distant resemblance to a paper cutter was used to cut off a tapering, narrow slice. The angle of the cut produced the point, while a hammer stroke or two, with the nail clenched in a vise, produced the head.

The cut nail is easily distinguished from the handwrought nail: even if it is rusting and deteriorated, it is usually discernable whether a nail tapers on all sides. If it does, it was handwrought. On a cut nail, only two sides taper. If the shaft is rounded, then the nail was made from wire, postdates 1850 at least, and probably was made after 1875.

AFTER THE CIVIL WAR

The economy of post-Civil War America was, for the first time in the nation's history, not based on agriculture. The United States was on its way to becoming one of the world's great industrial powers, and suburbs began to appear around such major industrial cities as Boston, Chicago, Los Angeles, and even Minneapolis and Omaha. The more comfortable half of the population could be described as "middle class," in that they could afford to own their own homes. The homes they got featured more and more factory-made parts.

Before the railroads and factories made it possible for so many goods to be shipped virtually anywhere in the land, it was invariably cheaper to buy local materials. As a result, most eighteenth-century houses were built with frames made of indigenous oak and with clapboards and shingles of local pine. The hinges and other hardware might well have come from England, but the bulk of the house was firmly rooted in the locality.

The machines producing standardized materials had a nationalizing effect. By the end of the nineteenth century, lumber for a typical house might still have been locally cut and milled, but the doors, the exterior trim, the hardware, and much else would be selected from a catalogue. The house built in New

AMERICAN GOTHIC:
1840–1875

This Gothic Revival house was featured in Andrew Jackson Downing's *Cottage Residences*. Its walls are protected with the board-and-batten siding he favored, and the design features a pair of front-facing gables (often there was a single, centered gable). The steeply pitched gables are decorated with elaborate vergeboards and the windows extending into them. The porch and front door are capped with Gothic arches.

Origins: The Gothic age of architecture in Europe, roughly the late twelfth through the fourteenth century, followed the Romanesque era and preceded the Renaissance, making it medieval. However, it was the English Gothic Revival of the eighteenth century that produced American Gothic. Architect Alexander Jackson Davis designed in the style as early as 1832, but its popularity began to spread rapidly with the publications, in the next decade, of Andrew Jackson Downing.

Shape: The style is distinguished by its "verticality," as the architectural historian would have it. Gothic stone cathedrals in Europe soared to extraordinary heights, and American Gothic buildings share the tendency to direct the eye upward

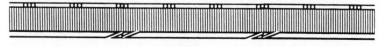

(though American Gothic houses are typically but one-and-a-half or two stories high). The roofs are steep, the gables topped with finials, and often the windows sweep upward to a characteristic pointed-arch shape.

Single-story porches were usual. For the first time in American architectural history, the floor plan (in perhaps a third of American Gothic houses) was asymmetrical, with an L-plan.

Details: Again, the emphasis is on the vertical. The characteristic "gingerbread"—elaborately shaped wooden decorative elements—was sawn into the bargeboards or vergeboards or stood up from rooftops. The inverted-V shape of the sawn barge-boards outlining a gable front is, along with one or more pointed-arch windows, the most telling identifying feature. American Gothic houses were most often built of wood, though brick and stucco are also found.

Doorways: The entry often had pointed arches or decorative headpieces.

Windows: The pointed-arch windows symbolize what we have come to think of as American Gothic. Often they had decorative trim sawn or carved into their headpieces. Sometimes lozenge (diamond-paned) windows were used, but 2/2 double-hung sashes were most common.

Location: American Gothic was largely a rural style. It was also relatively rare in the South, as the stately Greek style with its two-story portico was better suited to the climate.

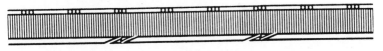

Hampshire might be indistinguishable from one constructed in California or Illinois, and all three had parts from factories across the country.

Styles were less regional, too, as a Queen Anne in San Francisco suddenly resembled one constructed in Boston or Chicago. Trends were national, like the one that made the porch a widespread (and peculiarly American) feature. In function, it is probably a variation on the overhanging roofs of French buildings in the West Indies and the Louisiana Gulf Coast. Called "galleries" (from the French *galerie*, for "long room"), these wide porches were found on French houses at the turn of the nineteenth century, but were a regional phenomenon.

The Victorian porch is also indebted to the Greek portico, but in Greek architecture (Classical and Revival) the roof loomed so high the space beneath wasn't shielded from the sun. In any case, by the mid-nineteenth century, the porch as we know it was a nationwide phenomenon found on houses of all styles. And not only on new houses, either, as innumerable older dwellings had porches grafted on.

In the same way, stained-glass windows had a Victorian vogue. The first stained glass in America was imported from Britain, and until the last quarter of the nineteenth century, little was made in the United States. Then, almost overnight, stained glass become widely popular. The decorative stained-glass sash was widely referred to as a "picture window."

Artist John La Farge is thought to have helped initiate the trend. He had visited England in 1873, and met Edward Burne-Jones and others of William Morris's circle who were working with handmade stained glass in a medieval manner. But it wasn't until late in the decade that La Farge translated an expensive British craft into a full-scale American business. As the story goes, La Farge was resting in his studio one afternoon when he observed the play of sunlight through the inexpensive glass of a tooth-powder jar on a window sill. From that inspiration, he went on to create windows of many colors and textures using inexpensive, mass-produced glass, glass quite different from the handmade material used in Great Britain.

In short order, stained-glass window sashes were no longer found only in the houses of the wealthy. By the 1880s, it was virtually standard for builders to incorporate simple, decorative stained-glass windows in new homes. The windows were not always pictorial or even elaborately patterned. Assemblages of simple squares or rectangles or diamonds of colored glass composed appealing fixed windows in the stairway, dining room, library, bay window, bathroom, or in the entryway transom, sidelights, or the front door itself.

Yet it isn't stained-glass windows, the balloon frame, or even the porch that best represents the spirit of Victorian architecture. It is, rather, the spirit of experiment, of change, of eclectic tastes in styles and colors. There was a willingness to try almost anything, and the diversity of styles of the age serve to underscore the point: there's Greek and Gothic, and the French Second Empire, and the Italianate, and the English-inspired Queen Anne. Yet for me, the octagonal house is a fitting standard-bearer for Victoria's century.

Orson Squire Fowler (1809–1887) was a phrenologist, perhaps the nation's best known practitioner of the "science" that claimed to be able to translate the pattern of bumps on one's skull into assessments of character and mental faculties. He published the *American Phrenological Journal and Miscellany* (which survived into the twentieth century), as well as other writings on health and sexuality.

Phrenology has gone the way of bleeding leeches, but Fowler did leave behind an architectural legacy. In 1848, he wrote a book titled *A Home For All,* in which he posited that the circle was nature's chosen building form. He pointed to its efficiency: it enclosed the greatest amount of interior space with the least exterior wall of any structural shape. Given the inherent difficulty of building circular structures (traditional building materials are virtually all rectilinear), he substituted the octagon as a practical alternative form. The octagon shares the advantages of the circle and is easier to construct. The octagon, he argued, was the most healthy and efficient form of building for air flow and well lit interiors. Apparently many of his contemporaries were won over by Fowler's arguments, as most prosperous nineteenth-century towns seem to have at least one octagonal house (usually along with a representative selection of the other, varied styles of the period).

The popularity of Fowler's octagon is to be judged on two grounds. The book went though at least nine printings between 1848 and 1858, which included a second, revised edition in 1853. The houses themselves had a nationwide vogue, as octagonal houses were built in nearly forty states. But the boom faded in the late 1850s, and his design has seen only occasional use in the years since. The octagonal house did not prove to be an enduring structural form.

Yet the progeny of Fowler's Folly (as his own octagonal house was known) represent more than a passing fad. The Victorians saw great social changes as an emerging middle class increasingly had the luxury to elevate its concerns from simple shelter to more abstract notions of beauty and truth. As the century wore on, the only architectural constant was eclecticism, a trait ably represented by Fowler's strangely appealing eight-sided houses.

AMERICAN BRACKET:

1840–1880

Pictured in an 1876 Genesse County, New York, atlas, this Italianate house is a high-style example of the American Bracket style. It has a square cupola, and brackets supporting the wide overhanging roof with very little pitch. The tall, narrow windows are 2/2s; the front entrance has a double door. The details that make this simple square box resemble an Italianate villa were often applied to other, more traditionally shaped double-pile, gabled houses.

Origins: It began with the villa style popularized by Andrew Jackson Downing, Alexander Jackson Davis, et al., based on English models. It's often considered separately as the "Italianate" style, but as William H. Ranless, another author of pattern books, said in 1851, the style "might with greater propriety be called the American-Italian, for it is more purely American than Italian in Character." (The many bracketed houses with cupolas are better termed "Italianate"; those with square or octagonal towers, "Italianate Villa".)

Between the years 1850 and the depression of 1873, American Bracket was the dominant style. Houses continued to be built in that style until about 1880, but gradually its place was taken in the public's taste by the Queen Anne house.

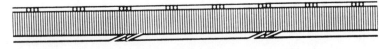

Shape: Two or three stories tall, houses in this style have a low-pitched roof with a broad overhang supported by the brackets that give the style its name. Along with the American Gothic, the Bracket house style did its bit to move the American house away from the symmetrical: not all, but many American Bracket houses had asymmetrical features like towers, ells, bay windows, balustraded balconies, and verandas. Almost all examples had porches.

Details: The brackets, of course, are a key clue, along with round-topped windows. The brackets came in any number of shapes and sizes, and usually were incorporated into the cornice and other moldings. Most American Bracket houses are made of wood.

Doorways: Double entrance doors are common and, for the first time, glass was incorporated into the door itself (rather than in a transom or sidelights).

Windows: Tall, narrow windows are the rule, often with arched or curved tops and carved or molded crowns. The sashes are usually 2/2s. Bay windows are common, as are adjacent pairs of round-headed windows.

Location: American Bracket houses are found in various guises in town and country alike. Perhaps the only part of the country without substantial representation is the South, although some examples are to be found there. The peak of popularity for the American Bracket style was the Civil War era and after.

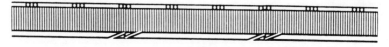

OCTAGON:

1850–1865

Here is Orson Fowler's philosophizing come to architectural life. This perspective drawing of the house, taken from the 1853 edition of Fowler's *A Home for All*, reveals the unmistakable configuration. The floor plan also suggests the equally distinctive room shapes the shape produced.

Origins: Perhaps more than any other style, the octagon is one man's brainstorm. Orson S. Fowler conceived the configuration as much as a philosophical matter as an architectural one (see discussion of Fowler, page 109).

Shape: It is, of course, the shape of the house that gives the octagon its name and that makes it

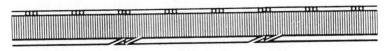

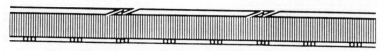

unmistakable. The octagonal house is eight-sided (though Fowler's writings did inspire a few six- and twelve-sided houses as well as a handful of round ones). Usually two stories tall, the octagonal house frequently was topped with a cupola and had porches on one or more sides.

Details: Octagonal houses were built with a wide variety of detailing. Some have Greek Revival moldings and pilasters, many have brackets, still others Gothicized bargeboards. Door and window treatments were generally symmetrical in layout, but their style tended to be consistent with the owner's or builder's choice of detail.

Interiors: As the floor plan from Fowler's book *A Home for All* suggests, the outer octagonal shape resulted in some rather unusual shapes inside. As a rule, the larger interior spaces assumed rectangular shapes, while the incidental rooms like closets and staff areas were more likely to have triangulated corners and peculiar proportions.

Location: Although relatively rare (perhaps only a few thousand were built), the octagonal house nevertheless can claim a notable and noticeable place in many a Victorian landscape. The distinctive shape is most common in the Northeast and Midwest. (In the 1960s and 1970s there was a brief vogue of octagonal buildings, but the methods of construction and absence of architectural detail should immediately distinguish the twentieth-century versions.)

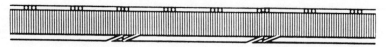

SECOND EMPIRE:

1860–1890

This Second Empire house (photographed ca. 1880), like many examples, has a square, boxy shape. But it is its mansard roof that identifies it. The bay windows on the first floor are common, the dormers on the third a constant in this style. The 2/2 windows and double front door are also the norm.

Origins: Although François Mansard, who gave his name to the roof configuration that identifies this house, died in the seventeenth century, it was the addition of Mansard-roofed wings to the Louvre in Paris between 1852 and 1857 that initiated this style. The era in France of the reign of Napoleon III (1852–1870) was known as the Second Empire, and it lent its name to the architectural style as well. At one time, the style was known as the "General Grant style" because of its frequent use here for public buildings during his administration.

Shape: The characteristic roof has two pitches on all four sides of a rectangular or square plan (some examples are ell-shaped, many have a tower at center front). From the peak, the roof line slopes at an al-

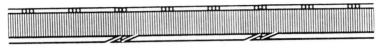

most-flat pitch, then suddenly becomes nearly vertical when it approaches the eaves (the flatter pitched part of the roof is usually not visible from ground level). Most often two stories tall, Second Empire houses usually have dormers that make the attic essentially a third floor.

Details: Brackets decorate the wide eaves; those and other details—window and door treatments, for example—resemble those of the American Bracket style. The roofs were often adorned with ornate ironwork and decorative slate shingling.

Doorways: Double entrance doors are quite common. Glass is incorporated in some houses into the upper panels of the door itself (rather than in a transom or sidelights).

Windows: Tall, narrow windows are the rule, often with arched or curved tops and carved or molded crowns. The sash are usually 2/2s.

Interiors: The style tends to an impressive verticality on the inside, with high ceilings and elongated windows to match. The sharply pitched roof and dormers also made the attic space livable, resulting in what was, for the time, a surprising amount of space in relation to the lot/floor area.

Location: Largely an urban style, the Second Empire house fits comfortably on narrow, in-town lots where light and space are limited. Today, in towns with a history of manufacturing growth in the third quarter of the nineteenth century, the General Grants remain, emblems of an early exploration of new-found wealth.

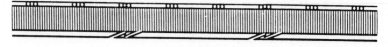

STICK STYLE:

1860–1890

Beneath the steeply pitched roof is the key decoration that distinguishes the Stick style house: the decorative trusswork. There's also the usual porch, and an intermingling of vertical and horizontal wall surfaces. This particular house was found in an 1883 plan book titled *Cottage Houses for Village and Country Homes*.

Origins: In a sense, this style is to be regarded as an outgrowth of the earlier American Gothic style. The Stick style owes a considerable debt to half-timbered medieval European styles, particularly given that Richard Morris Hunt, an American architect often credited with introducing the Stick style, studied in France at the time of a revival of half-timbered architecture in the restoration of medieval German towns.

Shape: In comparison to the complexities of the Queen Anne style house to follow, the shape of a Stick style house is simple. Plain gable roofs are the rule, often with a second cross gable, sometimes with a tower. The pitch of the roof is usually quite steep (though townhouse versions are flat-roofed),

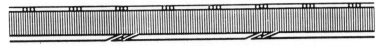

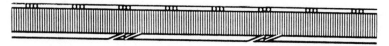

and a one-story porch typically lines the front of the two-story Stick style house.

Details: The Stick style is best recognized by the numerous horizontal, vertical, and diagonal wooden pieces applied to its wall surfaces. In fact, the Stick style is really an expression of wonder by its builders at the wealth of materials available to them. The carpenter was given free rein, especially on California examples. While there are handsome Stick style homes in the Northeast and elsewhere, it was on some of San Francisco's notable "painted ladies" that the style reached its zenith.

At the peak of the inverted-V of the gable, decorative trusswork is usually found; the walls are crisscrossed with a rectilinear pattern of wooden bands (the "sticks") that divide the shingled or clapboarded walls into a geometric pattern.

Doorways: Single or double doors were common, again with glass in the door itself rather than around its frame.

Windows: Long and narrow double-hung sash windows were the rule, either with 2/2s or single panes of glass.

Location: Never a dominant style like American Bracket or Second Empire or Queen Anne, with which it shared the second half of the nineteenth century, the Stick style was, nevertheless, an important decorative exercise, a working out, perhaps, of some experiments with suddenly plentiful materials and colors.

QUEEN ANNE:

1870–1900

Just as the buyers of the day saw it, here is a Queen Anne house from the 1900 catalogue *Shoppell's Modern Houses*. Note the hip roof with cross gables and the broad expanse of porch. Many examples also had bay windows, patterned shingles (see page 39), spindlework, and other decorations.

Origins: The so-called Queen Anne style really has very little to do with the English queen of the same name. She ruled from 1703 to 1714 but the style of architecture in vogue during her reign shares almost nothing with the American Queen Anne style house except that both blended Gothic and Renaissance elements.

The Queen Anne style of the last quarter of nineteenth-century America was a very free inter-

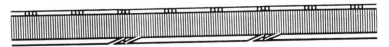

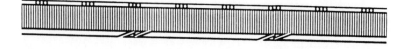

pretation of a contemporary English style that was already an interpretation of an amalgam of earlier English styles. Its American presence is often attributed to British buildings at the 1876 Centennial Exhibition. They were half-timbered designs, styles developed by Richard Norman Shaw in England in the 1860s.

Shape: Asymmetry is finally given full sway in the Queen Anne style. The steeply pitched roofs are highly irregular, with a complex blend of roof lines, dormers, gables, turrets, and tall, multiple chimneys. At the first-floor levels, asymmetrical porches add to the mix, and bay windows abound at both first- and second-floor levels. Usually, however, a single, front-facing gable dominates the Queen Anne façade.

Details: "Mix it up" must have been the motto of the Queen Anne builders. It seems the point was always to use as many different materials and textures on the same wall as possible. There are shingles and clapboards and moldings. There's half-timbering and terra-cotta panels and porches with spindles and brackets and finials and all kinds of ornamentation.

The profuse display wasn't limited to materials: the architectural details that lay at the heart of the

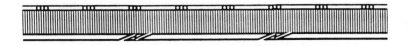

Queen Anne style were painted in such a way as to stand in relief to the rest of the building. Bold and bright and rich colors were used to great effect. When materials or forms changed, from shingles to clapboards to panels to moldings, the color changed, too.

Doorways: The doorway was usually a rather minor decorative element, set back onto the porch, though in some houses fan windows and sidelights appear. The door itself is generally single, though frequently with glass in its upper portion, often with stained glass set into it.

Windows: Windows vary greatly: Palladian, double-hung, round-headed, oculus (round), etc.; sometimes 6/6s were used. The protruding bay window, with rounded sides and a Palladian window on its front plane, is one hallmark of the Queen Anne style (though the Queen Anne was so broadly popular that there are many subtypes classifiable by shape and detail variations).

Location: In San Francisco, Boston, Iowa, and Texas; indeed, the Queen Anne had its day almost everywhere. Beware, even if your house is apparently Queen Anne, the style was so popular that many older houses were updated with turrets, bay windows, and porches.

SHINGLE STYLE

1880–1900

This large, comfortable-looking house is indeed shingled. Its porches, mixed rooflines, and Palladian window are also typical touches. According to the outfit that sold its plan, the Co-Operative Building Plan Association, this five-bedroom house would cost $3,500 to build. That was in 1890.

Origins: In the East it was H. H. Richardson and the firm of McKim, Mead and White; in the Midwest, Frank Lloyd Wright; in the West, Willis Polk. These architects and others built major houses in the Shingle style. Their work was based on their adaptation of what they saw in early American architecture: the simplicity of the unpainted siding and the gable roofs as contrasted to the ornateness of other contemporary styles.

Shape: Two or three stories tall, with a steeply gabled roof (or with several gables and intersecting roof lines) but with little overhang.

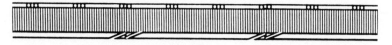

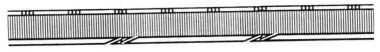

Porches are usual, and dormers are hipped or eyebrow. The gambrel roof was also used in some Shingle style houses.

Details: In comparison to the Queen Anne, Shingle houses seem lower. In some examples, the first floor is brick or textured stone. Originally the roofs were also shingled, though many have since been resurfaced with other materials. But most important, their shingle siding gives them an uncomplicated surface appearance.

Doorways: Simple treatments were the rule, with a minimum of adornments.

Windows: In keeping with the early American buildings that inspired these houses, the windows used were relatively small with numerous lights. However, they were often grouped in twos and threes and may be either casement or double-hung windows; Palladian and bay windows were not uncommon.

Interiors: Openness is the key. In these large houses, the spaces inside and out blend together.

Location: The earliest Shingle style houses were built in southern New England, but the style shortly moved to New York's Long Island, Maine, and other areas. Coastal settings seemed especially well suited to the style, though bucolic country locations became more common after widespread publicity for the style appeared in architectural magazines.

5.

INTO THE
TWENTIETH
CENTURY

1900–1930

The construction of ever larger buildings became possible in the nineteenth century, thanks to the invention of the elevator and the evolution of the iron frame (at mid-century). The steel-frame building replaced the iron-frame (at the turn of the twentieth century), and reinforced and prestressed concrete were also developed. Buildings and bridges of previously undreamt of size were constructed.

The single-family house was relatively unaffected by these changes. Early in the twentieth century the steel girder came into occasional use in basements to strengthen a long foundation span, and Frank Lloyd Wright and others used reinforced concrete in such spectacular structural feats as the Fallingwater House, in which Wright cantilevered an assortment of horizontal shapes over a waterfall. But since stick-built framing (see page 14) came into general use in the last quarter of the nineteenth century, the structure of the average American house has changed little.

Yet the elements of the structure are vastly different now. One economic fact speaks clearly to the point. At the turn of the nineteenth century, more than ninety cents of every dollar spent building a house were invested in its structure. By 1920, only about half of the cost of building a typical house was invested in its floors, walls, and roof—the rest went for site and mechanical equipment. The balance continues to shift further each year.

By 1927, three of five American homes had electricity; in the years following World War I, vacuum cleaners, electric dishwashers, and refrigerators become widely manufactured consumer goods. Because of central heating systems, a new house didn't have to be shaped like a box to assure adequate distribution of heat; it could be elongated or segmented. Electric lighting meant a room of any size or proportion—or any portion of any space—could be brightly lit.

Standardization grew ever more commonplace. The balloon- and platform-framing systems were made possible because virtually all lumber was cut to standard sizes (two-by-four inches, two-by-six inches, and so on). The lumber, when used for the frame of a house, was nailed with identical nails and in identical patterns whether the carpenter wielded his hammer in Indiana or in Georgia. Windows changed, too, and the 1/1 double-hung window with its large panes of glass has dominated twentieth-century construction. Some revival styles have used lattice or, more recently, mock grids to suggest separate lights, but the norm is one large clear sheet of glass per sash.

Yet not all of these moves to factory-made standards were universally regarded as positive. Some of these second thoughts led to the American version of the Arts and Crafts movement.

REMEMBERING THE HANDMADE

The movement began in England during the Victorian age, and thus is, in its English incarnation, a nineteenth-century phenomenon. William Morris and the critic John Ruskin and others began it in reaction to what they saw as the tyranny of the machine. Their goal was to reintroduce high-quality, handmade goods. The movement came later in the United States, roughly at the turn of the twentieth century, but on both sides of the Atlantic, the Arts and Crafts movement was a reaction to an increasingly mechanized world.

At the most obvious architectural level, it was a response to the gingerbread and other decorations characteristic of the many Victorian styles. Surface appearances—decorative brackets and cut shingles and polychrome painting schemes—were emphasized at the expense of the verities of the craft of building. Many styles had become mere sham, and the carpenter/joiner had been replaced by the mechanical worker, who did little more than assemble prefabricated parts.

The responsibility for the creative act of shaping the materials was gone, along with much of the responsibility for planning and considering the nature of the structure being built. The poor quality of much work offered little of the personal satisfaction characteristic of the days when every cottage was a farm and factory, and the produce of both was a matter of immediate necessity and, by extension, personal pride. In furniture and the decorative arts, there was a similar sense of being adrift in a sea of machine-made goods, and there was a move to simpler, often handworked shapes and textures and colors.

That summarizes the argument of the Art and Crafts movement, but there was an opposing force for it to contend with. Economic realities, as always in America, intervened. The growing economy after the turn of the century led to more people having more money to spend. The automobile, the telephone, the movie house, the consumer society changed people's lives. By the 1920s, for the first time more Americans lived in cities than in the countryside. It was a different world, and it required more and different houses. The mechanistic approach seemed to suit the situation better than the quality crafts approach (the middle class had money, but not enough to buy handmade houses).

Initially, the need for housing was met by the bungalow

on the West Coast and the houses of the Prairie School in the Midwest. In the East, it was the Colonial Revival in its various guises. Eventually, the foursquare and the bungalow and the Cape Cod all went national in mass-produced models, but they each owed a debt to the Arts and Crafts movement.

In 1898, a furniture-maker from Syracuse, New York, named Gustav Stickley traveled to England. There he came under the influence of William Morris and company. Stickley liked what he learned and, in 1901, founded *The Craftsman* magazine, which he published for the next fifteen years. In it, he promoted his philosophy: well designed and well made furniture was, according to Stickley, a moral imperative. He preached about natural materials, from cobblestones to unpainted woods. His furniture was simple, made of hand-finished hardwoods. He used wrought iron and brass and ceramic tiles. His favorite words were "simple" and "inexpensive" and "comfortable" and "convenient"—they described what he believed were the chief verities of house construction as well as furniture design. His magazine included drawings and floor plans for bungalows and other simple houses consistent with his philosophy.

Both the bungalow and the Prairie styles were characterized by natural materials used honestly. Interior wood surfaces were left unpainted. No attempt was made to obscure structural wood on the exterior, and rough surfaces like stone and stucco were displayed rather than obscured. In its heyday, Stickley's magazine attained considerable popularity. But it was its influence on a few individuals that made Stickley the father figure he is today. Among his followers were Frank Lloyd Wright and a manager or two at Sears, Roebuck and Company.

Wright, unlike the idealistic Stickley, who went bankrupt in 1916, was willing to acknowledge the importance of the machine. "In the Machine," said Wright in a famous speech he gave in 1901 at Hull House in Chicago, lay the "only future of art and craft." Wright, arguably America's greatest architect, was greatly influenced by *The Craftsman*. His earliest work had been in the Shingle style, but he shortly moved into what came to be known as the Prairie style. And it is that portion of his oeuvre, which was widely copied and imitated, with which we are concerned. Ironically, Wright in his later and even greater work was able to develop a remarkably hand-wrought style of designing, work so singular that few have successfully imitated it. He devised unique solutions to the problems presented by individual needs and sites and, unlike most designers and homeowners, had the luxury of carrying his house designs through to the last details. He designed chairs and tables along with the rooms in which they were to be used. His specifications for custom-made windows and numerous other details, inside and out, made his work less about shelter than about art. As a result, his chief value to the architectural student today is not as a source of specific shapes and visual ideas but as a problem solver: he devised his own solutions, always addressing the needs of the eye. He was able to carry out, for wealthy clients, what Stickley wanted the average man to be able to accomplish for himself. But Wright's early work was eminently practical.

Moving from the Shingle style, Wright went on to create—as no American had done before—an entirely new style of building. His inspiration was the geography of the style's birthplace. The buildings are low and long, with open rooms that appear as low and flat as the prairie. He flattened the roof and assembled windows into horizontal ribbons. Simple materials provided decorative touches: horizontal bands of wood trim or courses of brick were used to contrast the planes of a wall. As his style developed, he "broke the box," abandoning the rectangular symmetricality for T- and L-shaped buildings.

The most widespread Prairie style house, however, is perhaps the least revolutionary. The American foursquare is a simple, squarish structure with unadorned walls, a squat roof (with broad overhangs, of course), and usually a porch in front and dormers on top. The foursquare is, despite the extravagant beauty and genius of Wright's other work, his most enduring residential legacy. It seems only right that, having been influenced by *The Craftsman* early on, Wright's Prairie style, in the guise of the foursquare and other configurations, found its way into the pages of Stickley's magazine.

The foursquare peaked in popularity before and after World War I, along with another configuration of shorter stature but even greater popularity. To many, the bungalow was the American dream: it was small, yet its efficiency of design made it surprisingly comfortable. Its open plan made the limited space on the first floor seem more gracious. In the story-and-a-half versions, the bedrooms above were as small as the low ceilings in the eaves that contained them, but that configuration helped make the house affordable. The bungalow was frequently pictured and described in *The Craftsman*.

It wasn't only Stickley who helped the populace develop a taste for the bungalow. Popular magazines like *House Beautiful* and *Ladies' Home Journal* and *Country Life* spread the word, too. But it was Sears for whom the bungalow and the foursquare became bestsellers.

Between 1908 and 1940, Sears sold more than 100,000 houses; Sears wasn't the only company in the business, but they were by far the largest. Some of the houses sold in the Sears line of "Modern Homes" were large, some small. There were bungalows and foursquares and cottages and a miscellany of Colonial Revival types. Shipped by rail, precut and ready to assemble, the homes came complete with instructions and, if necessary, financing (a typical rate was 6 percent for a term of five years). Throughout the 1920s, bungalows dominated the pages of the Sears catalogue.

By no means all the houses of the early twentieth century were as "modern" as Wright's or the bungalow. The houses of the Colonial Revival, while eminently livable, were distinctly short on innovation. Some mimicked the center hall and squarish rooms of the Georgian double-pile plan, while others simply applied a Colonial finish to the then current Queen Anne layouts.

The year 1876, some say, saw the birth of the Colonial

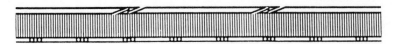

DISTINGUISHING
COPIES

If you think your house may be a copy of an old house, look to its hidden parts. It is rare in copying an antique house that the builders will go to the trouble of hand-hewing beams in the attic or basement. The cost would be great with no particular visual benefit.

That isn't to say that post-and-beam structures can't be found. In fact, they have gained popularity in the last decade. However, the timbers will probably be machine-shaped, either planed smooth or with visible circular-saw marks. Often nails are used as fasteners rather than wood pins. There may or may not be mortise-and-tenon joints. An antique house (that is, one built before ca. 1840) will have hand-hewn beams and mortise-and-tenon joints holding the frame together.

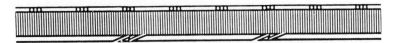

Revival. That was the year of the great Philadelphia Centennial Exhibition, at which an overwhelmingly popular attraction was the exhibit of a Colonial kitchen. As the story goes, the American past, in particular its furniture and household goods, were transformed in the eyes of the emerging middle class from attic anachronisms to symbols of a meaningful past.

In architectural terms, the year 1876 doesn't make sense, in that the activity didn't really begin in earnest until the 1890s, after the designers of Shingle style homes had set the pace. They built specifically Georgian Revival houses as well as their shingled experiments. Another major impetus for the

Colonial Revival movement came even later, in the 1920s, from John D. Rockefeller's restoration experiment at Williamsburg, Virginia.

For nearly a century now, numerous houses have been built in a conscious attempt to capture something of the practicality, good sense, and perhaps the aura of the Colonial dwelling. Only a handful of these Colonial Revival buildings are close copies of original structures, true in architectural form and detail if not in certain practical aspects (that is, modern bathrooms and kitchens have been de rigueur in the immensely popular Colonial Revival houses). Some of the best of the copies are so good that you must resort to nail, framing, and other material identification to be sure of their vintage. Relatively few are copies; rather, they use the language of Colonial buildings, so far as it was understood, but in a free-form improvisation.

The Cape Cod came back; so did the Dutch Colonial, though in so stylized a manner that its alleged progenitors would probably find it unrecognizable. There was a revival of numerous English styles that had never made an appearance on our shores before, from Cotswold to Tudor. The Spanish Colonial Revival had a variety of guises, among them the Pueblo and the Mission styles. But all were constructed as modern homes, the builders not forgetting for a moment the advances made in the modern era in the way of comforts and practicality.

CHANGING TIMES

In the nineteenth century, new nails and screws and cutting tools revolutionized the construction of houses. In the twentieth century, there were no such great individual leaps. There have been lots of small changes and improvements since World War II, like the advent of plastic plumbing, the widespread use of drywall construction, the introduction of drywall screws, nail guns, and super adhesives. The result has been houses that are built much more quickly, if not always better.

Perhaps the greatest single change in our century has been in the electrical system. By 1910, electric power was reliable, and booming, so that by the 1920s electric lighting was quite common. A General Electric study in 1931 determined that between 1920 and 1927, the number of outlets in the average six-room house went from twenty-one to *fifty-three*. Municipal electric utility systems served urban homes, and small private plants delivered power to many smaller towns and even rural areas. But farms only gradually received electric service over the next several decades.

Other changes in house-building were more a matter of fabrication. The goods were made differently, but the materials were much the same. Increasingly, wood paneling was made from precut boards with machine-made tongues and grooves. Despite the Arts and Crafts movement, standardization gradually became the rule in all the building trades: wire sizes, lumber and board dimensions, concrete blocks, plumbing fittings, all kinds of materials were made to national standards. After World War II, even the height of a kitchen countertop was standardized.

The introduction of gypsum board typifies these changes. Today, more than 90 percent of all new houses and apartments have gypsum board walls and ceilings, yet at the turn of the twentieth century almost none did. The shift didn't occur overnight and old-fashioned lath and plaster will never disappear entirely. But the stages in the transition are illuminating.

For more than two hundred years, wooden strips were the rule for supporting plaster. An inch or two wide and about three-eighths of an inch thick, the lengths of wooden lath were nailed horizontally to vertical framing members. Gaps were left between the strips. The first layer of plaster would ooze through the gaps forming "keys" which, upon hardening, would hold the plaster surface in position. (For a discussion of dating and identifying wood lath, see Chapter 4.)

At least two and usually three layers of plaster were required. The "scratch" coat was the first. It was rich in lime, and often cow hair was mixed in to strengthen the brittle plaster, reinforcing it against cracks caused by the inevitable flexing and movement of the structure over time. The "brown" coat was next, its sandy color and texture coming from the large amount of sand mixed with the plaster. The "finish" coat of smooth white plaster had no cow hair or sand.

Today, walls made with lath use "expanded metal lath." It is made from sheet metal by cutting a pattern of slits into it and then stretching. This machine process produces a series of openings. The layers of plaster are applied in the same way as with wooden lath, and the result is indistinguishable, at least on the day it's finished. Over time, however, the plaster surface supported by wooden lath shrinks slightly, and develops a gently undulating surface. To the trained eye, old plaster on lath can easily be distinguished from the mirror-flat surface of new plaster or plaster applied to metal lath.

That's the way lath-and-plaster walls are made. With the introduction of "rock lath" at the end of the nineteenth century, there was, for the first time, an option. A precursor to gypsum board, rock lath was a substitute for the supporting lath and the first coat of plaster. It came in factory-prepared panels that measured 16 inches by 48 inches. The sheets were attached to the studs, and the finish coats of plaster were applied directly to them. Rock lath saved time and, given its reasonable cost, money.

Gypsum board evolved slowly into the form we know today. Wet plastering remained the rule until after World War II, though prefabricated drywall was available a good deal earlier. (When I renovated my New York apartment, I found old gypsum board—also known as Sheetrock—on one partition. On it was a United States Gypsum Company label with a set of patent dates, the first of which was 1917. The last was 1927, leading me to conclude that the work on that partition wall was done in the late twenties.)

A man named August Sackett is usually credited with first combining plaster and paper to form a prefabricated plaster wallboard. His product, Sackett Plaster Board, came in 36-

by-32-inch panels, made up of four layers of paper and three of plaster (total thickness: 1/4 inch). It was weak and heavy, but it produced a wall so much faster and more easily than the lath-and-plaster process that it gained favor, especially after 1909 when Sackett sold out to United States Gypsum. Eight years and much experimentation later, they introduced Sheetrock. While plasterboard has had various guises (U.S. Gypsum wasn't and isn't the only maker) and it didn't catch on overnight, Sears, Roebuck and Company shortly offered it as an option on their kit houses.

The brand name Sheetrock and its competitors are also known as wallboard, plasterboard, and drywall (because it's applied dry, unlike wet plaster). Though hard on the back, hanging wallboard is not a skill that takes years to master, but, as with most shortcuts, there is a price to be paid. Gypsum board lacks the sound-proofing qualities of real plaster. As a building settles over time, the joints between the sheets of wallboard tend to reveal themselves and, unlike cracks in real plaster, aren't easily repaired with a cup of water and a bag of plaster. Some people don't like the texture of wallboard. If it is applied by careless workers, it can look sloppy.

Drywall, to me, represents the inexorable tide of change the American house has seen in its three-plus centuries. Traditional plaster and lath is prohibitively expensive for most homeowners, and it costs several times as much as drywall. Drywall is a trade-off that we have made: labor and cost have been saved, but the result isn't the same.

The change is a matter of materials and cost, but, perhaps more important, there is a skill factor, too. Even for those who can afford wet plaster walls, finding capable plasterers ranges from difficult to impossible, depending upon locality. The same is true for many other trades as well: the old skills have been largely lost, for economic and other reasons. That makes the surviving examples of the old ways, the classic older houses we are learning to cherish, all the more important.

BUNGALOW:

1903–1930

The bungalow had many variations, but this particular one was a Honor-Bilt Modern Home from Sears. Its Craftman origins are evident in the exposed rafters and the decorative braces that seem to support the roof. But it is the low-pitched gable shape and the porch, supported by its square piers, that make this house unmistakably a bungalow. *Credit: Sears, Roebuck.*

Origins: Charles Sumner Greene and Henry Mather Greene lived in Southern California, though they were graduates of the Massachusetts Institute of Technology. They also were trained carpenters and metalworkers. Their hands-on knowledge of materials and techniques enabled them not only to appreciate *The Craftsman* ethic but to act upon it.

They—and others—adapted the Hindu *bangla,* or "dwelling," especially a house of rest for travelers. Starting in 1903, the Greene brothers built an American incarnation of the Indian bungalow, one characterized by broad overhangs and porches.

Shape: The bungalow is a one- or one-and-a-half-story house with a gently sloping roof (usually

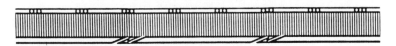

135

a gable, sometimes a hip roof) and small front veranda or porch. Dormers at the front and back are common. The porch roof is supported by tapering square columns.

Details: Structural roof members (rafter tails at the eaves and ridge pole at the peak) are exposed and sometimes decorated. Siding may be clapboard, shingles, or stucco.

Doorways: The doorways are simple, but the doors themselves usually have small glass lights in rectilinear arrangements.

Windows: Casement or double-hung windows have either single lights or multiple panes. Stained glass is sometimes used as a decorative element.

Interiors: The front door most often opens directly into the living room, and the interior space has an open feeling. The fireplace is a key element in the bungalow living room, usually made of stone or rough brick. Originally, many bungalows had unpainted wood trim though many homes have long had their woodwork painted.

Location: Thanks to wide publicity in magazines, the California or "basic" bungalow is found in other parts of the country, particularly in warmer climes where the shade provided by the eaves is a distinct advantage. The design lent itself to narrow, suburban lots. (The typical bungalow shouldn't be confused with "Western Stick" style, a high-style sub-variety of the generic bungalow.)

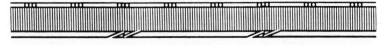

PRAIRIE SCHOOL:

1900–1920

This Frank Lloyd Wright perspective drawing was done ca. 1910 for a suburban subdivision. The broad expanse of its roof and wide overhang are typical; the two-story main building with one-story wing is also usual in the Prairie style. The ribbon of windows helps emphasize the essentially horizontal quality of the house.

Origins: Frank Lloyd Wright (early in his career) and other Chicago architects created the Prairie School.

Shape: The emphasis is on the horizontal, though Prairie School houses may be one or two stories high. The buildings parallel the prairie everywhere, with low-pitched hip, gable, or even flat roofs. Often the main section of a two-story Prairie School house has a hip roof, with perpendicular, single-story projecting wings (the floor plan, as a

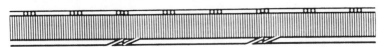

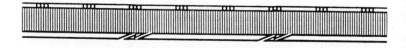

result, is T- or L-shaped). The chimney is large and low, positioned at the axis where the roof planes meet. Terraces, balconies, and exterior walks give the house an expansive, indoor-outdoor aspect.

Details: Usually built of brick or wood with the exterior most often of masonry or stucco. The most notable quality of the Prairie School house is the broad overhang of the eaves that enhances the low-to-the-ground quality of the design.

Doorways: The doorways are simple, but the doors themselves usually contain small glass lights in rectilinear arrangements.

Windows: Windows are casement or double hung, either with a single light or multiple panes of glass. Stained glass is sometimes used as a decorative element, as are clerestory windows.

Interiors: Fewer, larger rooms are the rule. Many "rooms" are separated not by doors but by broad openings. Bedrooms and baths are usually located on the second floor.

Location: Though found across the country, most examples are found in the Midwest.

COLONIAL REVIVAL:

1890–Present

Origins: The architects at the influential New York firm of McKim, Mead and White, the 1876 Centennial Exhibition, an emerging sense of America's self-worth, and a need to understand what once was in a time of overwhelming change; all are factors in the Colonial Revival. The Colonial Revival consists of numerous variations, of which the Georgian is probably the best known.

Shape: The houses of the Colonial Revival were not copies but immitations of eighteenth-century originals, updated to the technology and taste of another time. Incorporating the latest in creature comforts, including multiple bathrooms, well equipped kitchens, and electrical systems, these houses tend to be spacious and well constructed.

THE GEORGIAN REVIVAL: Built of wood or masonry, the Georgian Revival house generally has some of the detailing characteristic of its period inspiration. However, the quality of the work falls off considerably in houses built during and after the Depression.

They are two or three stories tall with a symmetrical shape and hipped, gable, or gambrel roof.

Doorways: Elaborate doorways are usual, often with a balconied portico in front and pilasters or sidelights.

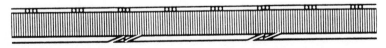

This Georgian Revival house, from *Modern American Homes,*
a 1913 catalogue, makes its twentieth-century origins evident immediately. The combination windows of the first
story give it away. (Rather than separate, double-hung sashes, there are three adjacent sets on each side of the front
door.) The front door, with its pilasters and decorative
headpiece, is also elaborate and a focus for the whole design.

Windows: Frequently the key clue in distinguishing the imitation from the original Georgian:
while the windows may have multiple lights, often
1/1 or 12/1 windows were used on Georgian Colonial
Revival houses. Other Victorian details such as bay
windows and stained glass also were incorporated.

Interiors: The floor plans vary a great deal; symmetry was usually maintained for the hall and for
the matching chimneys, though often room configurations are not strictly symmetrical.

THE DUTCH COLONIAL: As with the Georgian
Revival house, the Dutch Colonial Revival was inspired by Colonial dwellings as seen through twentieth-century eyes. The Dutch Colonial Revival
house is usually less pretentious than the Georgian;

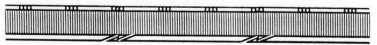

This Dutch Colonial house came as a kit from Sears. Named the Van Page to suggest its Lowlands ancestry, it is the gambrel shape of the roof and the so-called "Colonial sidelights" flanking the front door that justify calling the house "Dutch" and "Colonial," respectively. *Credit: Sears, Roebuck.*

it is a smaller, more modest house with its upstairs rooms built into the steeply pitched gambrel roof.

THE CAPE COD: In its most common configuration, it's the five-bay Cape back in business—a house with a door at the center flanked by two pairs of evenly spaced windows (see page 71 for Style Notes on the eighteenth-century Cape Cod house). Clapboards, shutters, center chimney—the echoes are there, as are the efficiencies of the original one-and-a-half-story design. The Cape Cod in its Colonial Revival package typically has a less steeply pitched roof than its inspiration, and the revival Cape may also have roof dormers on the front or a flat-roofed shed dormer across the back. Seldom seen in antique

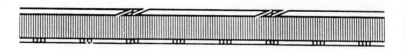

This Spanish Colonial Revival home is in San Jose, California. Built in the 1920s, it features the tile roof, stucco walling, and arched entrances characteristic of some Colonial Spanish homes—along with the garage and piping of its own time. *Credit: HABS*

New England Cape houses, the dormers add usable space to the second floor. The twentieth-century Cape often has a garage added at the side.

THE SPANISH COLONIAL REVIVAL: Inspired by the architecture of early Spanish settlements in Florida and the West, the Spanish Colonial Revival was popular in California (especially among Hollywood stars), in Florida (after World War I), and in the Southwest (especially a variation known as the Pueblo style, with earthen walls and a flat roof). The Spanish Colonial Revival house is usually built of stone or brick masonry that has been finished with stucco or plaster. Archways are usual, often in contrasting red brick or red tile. Tile roofs are of red clay, too, and ornamental wrought-iron balcony rails or decorations are also common.

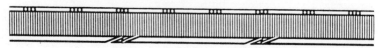

The enduring popularity of the Cape Cod house is suggested by this contemporary rendering from a seller of house plans. It's the five-bay Cape, all right, with garage addended. The center chimney is gone and five dormers have been added, but the classic good sense of the story-and-a-half design remains unmistakable. *Credit: Home Planners, Inc.*

Perhaps the most significant long-term effect of the Spanish Colonial Revival was the introduction of the patio, which in post-World War II America replaced the porch in many homes, regardless of the style of the house.

Location: Initially limited to the northeastern United States, the Georgian and Dutch and Cape Cod styles soon spread across the country. Their longevity, however, proved to be much greater in the East. To this day, the Cape Cod and the Dutch Colonial, as well as the Georgian (often simply called the "Colonial") are the staples of many mail-order plan companies, along with, in recent decades, the saltbox and other early American shapes.

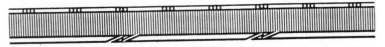

6.

THE
PAPER
TRAIL

Y ou can't believe everything you read. On the other
hand, a document of evident age and authenticity
is often the best single source of information about your house.
It can also provide a basis for further research into stylistic
matters and for the search for physical evidence.

In this chapter, we will look at sources of documentary
evidence. Some, like deeds and property tax rolls, are a matter
of public record and are primary sources, so it makes sense to
begin with them. Other potential sources are newspapers and
previously conducted research by writers and historians. The
latter are often best used to corroborate your primary sources,
but both are interrelated.

Keep in mind that you are trying to develop a broad
overview of the history of your house. It isn't only the day of
its construction that is important. The denizens of the house
and their travails over the decades may illuminate some aspect
of it, so it may be worth learning the vital statistics of previous
owners, too, such as when they were born and died, who they
married, what they did for a living.

Not every source will provide you with information, so you must be persistent in your search. As you assemble the seemingly disparate pieces, keep in mind that it is often the smallest clues that deliver the biggest discoveries.

THE PUBLIC RECORD

It is a "matter of public record," as the saying goes, if a document is made or gathered by the government. The public records available and of potential value to you in your investigation are many, ranging from deeds to wills, and include documents about construction, taxes, and mortgages.

The place to begin is with a "deed search" of your property's history of transactions. Public land records are supposed to cite owners back to the very first purchase of the land, though sometimes the records prove incomplete or the handwriting illegible. Nevertheless, a deed search is the first step in looking for paperwork clues to your house.

Deeds and Plat Maps: A legal description of property identifies a parcel of land. Commonly, the "metes and bounds" (measurements and boundaries) will be specified using compass readings and natural landmarks. Plat maps and deeds are the official documents that provide the "legal description."

A *plat map* is a plan of an area indicating locations and boundaries of individual properties (as distinct from a site or plot plan, which is a smaller drawing of a single piece of property). The plat map is usually found at your town hall or county surveyor's or tax assessor's office.

There will be plat maps from previous as well as current tax years, so you should be able to trace back the shifts in ownership not only of your plot but of those nearby. Long-term patterns of development may well emerge from a careful study of the tax plat maps.

Plat and plot maps are made on the basis of surveyors' field notes. The methods used for topographical measurement have varied greatly over the years. On many old records, such units of measurement as "links" (one link equals 7.92 inches) and links of "chains" (100 links make a chain) are used. They date from the early Public Land Surveys conducted under the terms of the Public Land Act of 1785. However, in the twentieth century, most surveying has been in feet (and in decimal portions thereof).

A legal description of a piece of property remains in effect until it is superseded by a new one. New descriptions (and surveys) are usually conducted only when necessary, such as to settle a dispute or at the time a piece of property is subdivided. If your house is located on a piece of property that hasn't been subject to such changes or challenges in this century, you may find yourself dealing with antiquated terminology. If necessary, consult with a professional surveyor or title insurance company for assistance.

A *deed* signifies ownership and thus is a key to who holds (or held) "title" to a piece of land and the buildings on it. Since title involves ownership of land (rather than buildings), a title search generally won't provide you with descriptions of how many or what sort of buildings were on the land when the deed changed hands. But it will tell you who bought and sold your property and when.

When you purchased the property, you and the mortgage holder may well have obtained a "property abstract." This document lists the previous title holder (at least), and also cites relevant mortgages, deeds, wills, liens and other litigation activities, and tax sales. However, it is the names of previous owners that are the keys to opening other doors. Using them, you can investigate tax records, wills, and other documents.

You may hire a title examiner or abstractor to conduct a search for you, though many people find this archival variety of detective work to be an informative bit of time travel. Keep in mind that, as television detective Jim Rockford never tired of telling us, good detective work isn't all hunches and car chases—there's a fair amount of library work, of looking through the records down at your city hall, and of knocking on doors.

146

Start by checking with the county clerk to find out where the records are kept. In most states, it is the responsibility of the county clerk, but in others (like Vermont and Connecticut) the town clerk handles the job. In either case, you must go to the archive. If the records haven't been put on microfilm, it's probably a good idea to go armed with tissues in case the dust awakens allergies you didn't even know you had.

Work backward. These records are kept chronologically, so find the entries for your date of purchase. The records should be indexed by both the grantor and grantee of the property (that is, the seller and buyer, respectively, either of whom can be corporations, groups, nonprofit organizations, or governmental bodies as well as individuals).

If you are lucky, you may discover descriptions of the buildings on the property (the chances are relatively small, however, as it has never been standard practice to include such descriptions). If you're unlucky, you may find yourself at a dead end because of a missing page or illegible handwriting. But you should expect to find the dates of sale and recording, as well as the dates of court cases, probate settlements, and perhaps even insanity hearings. Records of mortgages, liens, and bankruptcy will also be on the record. You may come across a "reconveyance," which means the property owner paid off a mortgage.

Mechanics liens are a rare but sometimes fruitful find. Since 1833, the construction industry has used them to get payment for services rendered, and upon occasion such liens have contained more substantial details about the work done and materials used (but, allegedly, not paid for).

Collect all the information you can, including the names of grantors and grantees, dates, mortgages or covenants, prices, and other specifics. References to earlier deeds or sales may be helpful in taking the next step back in time. Be sure you record the volume and page number where the records are to be found in case you ever want to take another look.

Go back in time again, using the grantor in your purchase. He will have been the grantee in the previous one. Then go

147

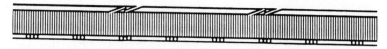

DOCUMENTARY SOURCES

When pursuing sources of printed history for your house, the following should be stops *en route:*

County Records Office: This office is the likely source for deeds, will extracts, mortgages, liens, tax records, and building permits.

Probate Office: When it's wills or inventories you seek, the probate office is your best source.

City Hall: Generally the local building department is to be found at the town hall, as are annual reports, property tax records, and plat maps.

Local Libraries: Among other sources of help found here should be city directories, local histories, and social registers or "blue books." Often, more general guidance is to be found, too, about other potential sources of material.

Historical Societies: Historical societies vary enormously in age, collections, and quality, but potential finds include cemetery records, local histories, architectural surveys, miscellaneous manuscripts, correspondence and other private papers, photographs of local interest as well as drawings and other artwork, publications of various kinds, and perhaps old tax records, wills, inventories, genealogies, and local directories.

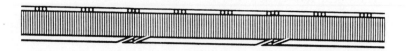

back again, and again, and again, if necessary. Chances are you'll find the years pass more quickly the further you get back in history, as the habit of moving frequently is a modern American phenomenon.

If the ownership of a property was transferred by inheritance rather than sale, you may need to check probate records; that could explain a break in the chain.

If you find evidence that the property was subdivided, follow that lead, too. Even if your house wasn't on the piece that was parceled off, another building might have been. It is possible, in any case, that you will be led to another source of information.

If you travel back far enough, you may just discover that the grantor was an English king (on the East Coast) or the United States government (in the case of federal land grants).

Wills: Like deeds, probate records are usually found at the county clerk's office. They are especially important when an owner dies. His or her will may yield a great variety of clues, including who inherited the house. Note other heirs in the will, as they or their descendants may be sources, too.

Like deeds, wills are usually indexed by last names. Along with wills, you may be fortunate enough to find administrator's accounts or an inventory. An inventory was often prepared when the owner died intestate (that is, without a will), and this can be an invaluable tool in learning about a house and its contents at a moment frozen in history.

Inventories list, for the purposes of the record, all of the deceased's worldly goods, complete with furniture and other valuables. Such lists can provoke a great deal of valuable speculation and are often used as the basis for restoring historic houses to the appearance they are thought to have had at specific times. Conclusions can be drawn about the financial status of the dearly departed, along with informed hypotheses about his or her work, home life, and even personal habits. If andirons are listed for a room, chances are it had a fireplace; the presence of but one bedstead in an inventory suggests that its location was the master bedroom. Historians have probably learned more about life in earlier eras from room-by-room inventories than from any other single source.

Some wills contain lengthy histories of the property being conveyed. Some offer clues to the buildings and their proprietors. A reference to a blacksmith's shed tells you something very specific about the work conducted on that property.

Wills can also confirm other findings or hypotheses. Suppose your house has an ell that was added after the original house was completed. If the hardware used on the doors leads you to believe it was built around 1850 and you discover through researching wills that the family who lived there had a child a year between 1847 and 1853, you might reasonably conclude your original conjecture was an accurate one.

Tax Records: Taxes are levied on the basis of assessed value, both of the land and the buildings on that land. They are a matter of public record.

Locate property and other tax records. Typically, twentieth-century records are at city or county offices, while earlier records are often in historical societies. Tax records should indicate the taxpayer of record (namely, the owner or his trustee), the tax rate, and the tax paid.

Traveling back in time via tax records will, at least for recent tax years, provide indications as to when increased taxes were assessed for improvements, providing clues as to when additions or renovations were done. An increase in total taxes may not indicate a change, but a significant change in a property's assessed value may. However, you should double-check with other properties in the community to rule out the possibility that an increase was simply a product of an across-the-board rate change.

Construction Records: Building permits are now required in most communities for any structure, including houses. In some urban areas, this has been so for a century or more, though the records are not always maintained. In some rural areas, such systems still do not exist.

Building department archives have been known to yield only filing dates, but in other instances a wealth of information has been found. In general, dates, materials used, the estimated cost, and the architect and/or contractor/builder are recorded. Other data may include the dimensions of the building, the construction schedule, and information about plumbing or electrical inspections. If you are very fortunate, you may find detailed architectural plans, though the odds are very much against finding any such drawings if the house predates the twentieth century.

Even if your house was built well before such records were kept, the building department files may still yield valuable information about later remodelings or additions. Public utilities may maintain records that reach back far enough to tell you when the place was electrified or given access to the municipal water supply.

Even if what you find seems trivial, when it is combined with other sources of evidence, surprising conclusions may emerge. A tax-rate increase and a building permit issued in the same year suggest a substantial addition. Perhaps that coincidence can provide the impetus to search out physical evidence that a portion of your house is not original. Record even the smallest, most confusing clues. They may make sense later.

OTHER SOURCES

Historical Societies: There are literally thousands of historical societies in the United States. They tend to have collections of general interest, with a particular emphasis on local matters. If the town was originally agricultural, you may find a vast array of farming implements; if the city was industrial, there may be machines or examples of the products made.

In addition, archives and files are usually kept on famous persons from the town, notable families, and general subjects, including architecture. In fact, many local historical societies in this country started because of local interest in preserving an old house.

The meetinghouse on the left is gone, but the stately Georgian home in the foreground and other buildings still survive today. This painting, the work of Deacon Robert Peckham, provides valuable clues about the ca. 1845 appearance of this Massachusetts main street. *Credit: Westminster Historical Soceity*

If there's an historical society in your town, go and visit it and become a member. Membership fees are usually small, and newcomers are almost always welcome.

Census Records: Starting in 1790, the federal government began taking a national census every ten years, identifying the heads and size of households and, in 1850, the names of all the members. The occupation of the head of the household was also recorded. You may find census records for your town or county at the local county clerk's office, and those up through 1900 may offer much valuable information. If not available locally, all census records are on microfilm in the National Archives in Washington, D.C. For property that was used for agricultural purposes, other useful information may also be found in census records.

Local Newspapers: Although most newspapers are not indexed, there are several major-city papers, including *The New York Times* and *The Washington Post,* that are. They can provide insights into issues of national significance.

Local newspapers are more likely sources of information germane to your research, and local libraries may well have compiled indexes and developed other means of easy access to back issues. Simply by reading newspapers published around the time your home was built, you may get some idea of the household goods and decorating materials being used at that time in your area. Advertising, in particular, often offers a surprisingly representative look at the consumer tastes of the day.

Using what you learned from other sources, try to learn more. If you know when a one-time owner of your house died, look up his or her obituary. You may learn something about the house specifically or, more likely, uncover further leads about relatives (survivors or ancestors) or about his or her business. Learning about the owner's profession or family may help explain one oddity or another about your house or its configuration. A second street entrance, for example, might have been useful for a widower father sharing his house with his daughter's family or for a lawyer practicing at home.

City Directories: In the days before phone books, most municipalities had compilations of names and addresses and occupations of most adult residents. They were published annually in larger communities, less often in smaller towns. They can be invaluable in following the occupancy of a house.

Start with more recent editions and work backward. If you already know who lived in your house in, say, 1925, consult the directory for that year and find the owner. If you don't know the name, use the street index. Not all, but many twentieth-century city directories have them. Then work backward to trace earlier residents. You may be able to trace the year of arrival or departure of previous owners. Their previous or successive residences elsewhere in town may provide other clues.

Your house may not be listed. If it isn't, it may not have been built at that time. If you know it existed, the street numbering system may have changed. In that case, try tracing other houses nearby. Other possible explanations are that the house was a rental, owned by a single woman, or, if there was a fee required for inclusion in the directory, as there was in some localities, the then-residents elected not to pay it.

Church Records: Churches often have records that go back to the founding of the parish. Membership information can be helpful, as can dates of baptisms and marriages. Some church files contain quite extensive details about their parishioners.

Local Histories: Check at your local library or historical society (community, county, or state) to determine whether there are any publications concerning local history. Over the last century, there have been several vogues in such history writing, notably during the Colonial Revival at the turn of the century and during the Depression when the Federal Writers' Project of the Works Progress Administration funded a number of state and local historical works. The 1976 bicentennial celebration instigated another spate of local historical publications.

Some works are specifically architectural. The U.S. Department of the Interior has made available matching grants for architectural surveys (in Connecticut, for example, more than 80 of the 169 towns in the state have had architectural survey maps prepared since the middle 1970s). Some of these surveys describe specific houses on the basis of considerable research, so several pages of material about your house may be available to you. In such cases, you may find much of the paperwork has already been done. Most of these publications, however, are more general, focusing on the history of the town, its important citizens (who may well have funded the projects in return for biographical attention), or key events in local history. Some of these books are surprisingly well written and may offer valuable clues in your search.

Don't overlook the possibility of academic publications concerning your city or region. Check with the libraries at local colleges, especially if there are urban studies or American studies degree programs there. Some dissertations may provide not only useful information, but their extensive bibliographies can offer further leads.

Registers of Historic Places: Chances are that if your house is on the National Register of Historic Places, you already know it. If it is, it will be worth your while to examine the records at your state historical commission. Buildings included on the register are described in detail, and historical background, including the names of previous owners, the architect, builder, and other significant information is likely to be found. In some cases, the files also include some structures that have been surveyed but not yet nominated.

Your state or municipality may also have a registration program for homes. A building doesn't necessarily have to have been the home of a famous person, or even to be of surpassing architectural quality. Many lesser houses are cited on the federal and state registers either on their own merits or as part of an historic district.

PICTORIAL RESOURCES

At some time or other, virtually every inch of the United States has been mapped. That mapping consists not only of plat maps prepared in conjunction with real estate transactions, but a variety of other map sources as well.

Beware of interpreting the appearance of a house on a map as absolute evidence of its age, since new buildings were often built on the foundations of old ones. On the other hand, a house may be older than its foundation, since in the eighteenth and nineteenth centuries houses were moved more often than they are today. However, the estimated age of a house can often be confirmed by reviewing official maps of a town. If the house doesn't appear on one map but does on the one prepared ten years later, it is reasonable to take that as corroborative evidence of its era of construction.

Geological Survey Maps: One source of recent maps is the United States Geological Survey. There are maps available from the USGS for every locality in the entire country. These maps show the topographical characteristics—hills and valleys, stream beds and roadways—as well as the individual structures in the area represented. While they are not likely to provide clues about earlier eras, they are used by the National Register to designate formally the location of buildings, and they can also provide a basic, current, correct reference when reviewing other maps. Aerial photography is used to periodically update the USGS maps. They are available from the local USGS office or your state's geological bureau for only a few dollars each.

Insurance Maps: Between the mid-nineteenth and mid-twentieth century, maps were published by and for insurance companies for use in writing fire insurance policies and adjusting claims. The business began in eighteenth-century England, but it didn't take off in this country until after the Civil War.

The most successful producer of these specialized maps was the Sanborn Map Company. Founded in 1867 by D. A. Sanborn, a surveyor from Somerville, Massachusetts, the company had produced maps of 11,000 communities by 1924. The maps featured street layouts and houses, but through the use of color keys and other systems also specified such building characteristics as size, construction and roofing materials, the number of stories, porches, and outbuildings.

The insurance-map business faded from prominence during the Depression, but if maps were made of your community, local libraries or title insurance companies are the most likely sources for them. You may also find them in the files of local fire companies, who were usually provided with copies, or discover that they were passed on to the local historical society.

The Library of Congress has a collection of over 700,000 Sanborn maps in its Geography and Map Division.

If you find insurance maps for your town, start with a map that dates from twenty or thirty years *after* the estimated construction date of your home and work backward. These maps were updated periodically (five and ten years intervals are common, though major fires required unscheduled revisions). If your house appears on one map but is missing on the previous one, that suggests it was built in the intervening years.

Other Maps: Your local historical society may have prepared map materials for its own purposes, or it may have in its collections a variety of maps from which a great deal can be learned about the town, including when trains first came through, when major highway work was done, or when factories or other industrial activities commenced.

Photographs: Short of architectural drawings, the single best source of evidence about the appearance of a house is a photograph. Even a picture of somebody else's grandpa can be invaluable—if his house can be seen in the background, perhaps with its long-destroyed porch still intact.

Photography was an infant art in the 1850s, and relatively few photographs remain from the early decades of photography, especially of the homes of simple folk. However, when the Kodak box camera came into more general use in the 1890s, a wealth of valuable documentation began to accumulate.

As usual, finding these photographs is the challenge. Previous owners are the best sources, but others are local libraries, historical societies, and newspapers. Don't overlook the potential value of older photographs of other, similar houses in town. They may have been built simultaneously or even by the same carpenter as yours.

If you were an early fan of the public television series "This Old House," perhaps you remember the Mansard-roofed Victorian with which the show began. Before host Bob Vila

The odds are great that this house looks a good deal different today. Perhaps it now has an addition or two, and that apple tree was probably burned in the woodstove years ago. Yet even when this photograph was taken before the turn of the century, there was a story of change to be read. Note that there are 12/12, 6/6, and 2/2 windows. If you bought this house tomorrow, this photograph might be very useful in considering your approach to restoration/preservation.

and the crew of cameramen and carpenters performed their renovation, they did some research.

They discovered who the original owner was and that the house was built in 1864. They learned of a 1939 renovation conducted by the former owner, a doctor, in order to provide a separate entrance for his at-home offices. In the spirit of that time, the style was Colonial Revival. But the best find of all was a packet of photographs that arrived via the U.S. Postal Service from Maine.

The photographs were taken by members of the family that had lived there in the 1920s. They showed what the house had looked like in those years, both inside and out. The furniture was different, of course, as was the wallpaper and the windows at the front of the house. There was a vine-covered trellis in the yard and a monster cast-iron cook stove in the kitchen.

YOUR PAPERWORK

As the chief historian and restorer or preserver of your home, you have a responsibility to maintain your own written records. You'll need the guidance of your sheaf of drawings and notes if you do any restoration work on the house. There is also a growing feeling among owners of older houses, many of them frustrated by the lack of such records, that they owe it to posterity—especially to future owners—to maintain such records.

The House Diary: You will need to keep scrupulous records of various kinds as you make changes and apply for building permits and calculate your taxes, but even before you remove one nail or square inch of wallpaper, you should begin keeping a casual, personal written record of the house.

Buy a blank manuscript book. Keep it beside your bed or in the top drawer of your desk—someplace where you can conveniently, and regularly, record what's done, by whom, and your observations about the work. You don't have to write in it every day; you don't have to write in full sentences. In fact, you may chose to write little and draw a great deal. Another option is a ring binder in which a great variety of materials can be collected and organized.

You must, however, start it when you really start—that is, not when you start restoring but when you start *thinking* about restoring. It is perhaps most essential to keep it during any demolition. Even if you hire others to do the demolition, make sure you're there when it's done. Alert the fellows with the plaster dust in their hair and little white masks that you want a running commentary on what they find. If you're lucky, you may find a demolition contractor or a laborer who has an active mind and notices things and has a certain perspective on what he sees because he's seen lots of buildings come apart before.

Don't write only about what you know, but record your questions, too. Just because *you* don't understand a reference in a deed or the pattern of the nail holes doesn't make it less of a clue.

Keep the diary throughout the process. You'll find yourself referring back to early pages to assist your memory as you are reassembling what had to be removed earlier. And don't consign the diary to a dusty, high shelf when you're "finished." No house, old or new, is ever really completed.

The House Files: Over the course of your investigations, you may assemble a substantial variety of notes, photocopies, correspondence, maps, drawings, and other paperwork. There are only two important rules: First, save those records, and, second, file those records.

To start with you won't need a filing cabinet, but do yourself the service of beginning with at least a few file folders. Some logical divisions might be "Deed Search," "Interview Notes," "Architectural Drawings," and so on. Open new files as you need them, and be sure to have a designated storage space for these records.

The House Pictures: If you're not a photographer, it's time you learned. With the equipment available today, anyone can take a photograph, and when it comes to recording physical evidence, there's no substitute for photographs. Although color pictures are useful in some instances, they do not have the permanence of black and white photos.

Don't skimp on pictures as you work on your house. They are invaluable for reference later: once a wall is gone, there's no way you'll be able to remember all the details of its construction without photographs or drawings of its parts. Take too many pictures: the cost is minor, and later on you will be glad you have them either for reference or perhaps for a scrapbook chronicling the restoration.

A CASE HISTORY

The place is a charming surprise. In New York City, where twenty-story apartment buildings are the norm, the little two-story houses have a small-town scale. They have an Old World quality, too, constructed as they were in a quasi-Tudor Revival style of half-timbered façades mixed with brick and stucco.

It's called Pomander Walk, and got its name from a London street and a Broadway play of the same name. The little buildings don't face onto a busy city street, but rather look at one another across a 24-foot-wide private sidewalk. Decorated with small gardens of flowers and privet hedges, the walkway bisects the city block, closed at its ends by iron gates facing onto West Ninety-fourth Street at the south end and West Ninety-fifth Street on the north.

To assemble the story of a typical, rural farmhouse, the best sources are likely to be deeds and plat maps. But in the case of a unique place like Pomander Walk, not only the sources but even the goals of an investigation may be quite different. Establishing when Pomander Walk was built is easy, since a stone rests atop the Ninety-fifth Street entrance, with the date 1921 carved into its surface, along with the names of the then-owner, Thomas Healy, and the architects, King and Campbell.

The need to research the original finish and configuration of the place is minimal. The exteriors of the buildings, through neglect of a not entirely benign variety, have been almost entirely unchanged (even the original bright colors have been retained). Some interiors have been modified, but enough of the apartments remain as they were that there is ample opportunity to see original moldings, wall and floor surfaces, and even original and antiquated sinks and high-legged gas ranges.

In the case of Pomander Walk, the point of an investigation is not so much a matter of looking for hard information for restoration purposes as it is a softer search for more ephemeral matters. One can find, at the New York City Buildings Department, the application for the certificate of occupancy. Dated December 15, 1921, it was granted on January 25,

In the foreground, it's Pomander Walk, a quiet surpise and
sharp contrast to more typical Manhattan apartment buildings (like the towering structures beyond). The scale and
detailing are right out of Tudor England.

1922. In a newspaper article (found via *The New York Times
Index* for 1921), I learned that as of April 24th of that year,
"Thomas Healy . . . holds from the Higgins estate a 200-year
lease on the property." Higgins, other articles revealed, bought
the property in the nineteenth century.

More interesting, however, is that Healy apparently had
a particular fondness for the theatrical world. In addition to
borrowing the design for the façade from a fashionable show,
he rented apartments to numerous performers. It is said that
Madeleine Carroll, Lillian Gish, Humphrey Bogart, and Ros-

alind Russell have all been among the many notable one-time residents of Pomander Walk.

The play *Pomander Walk* is of interest, too. It's a comedy about a young man and woman who meet and fall in love, only to discover that, many years before, his father and her mother had done the same thing. It's a light entertainment, with love conquering all in the end.

The play, like Pomander Walk itself, was something of an escape. Its prologue announced, "Kind friends, to-night we lead you far away / From all the turmoil of the busy day," a sensation one shares upon stepping into the quiet, private walk from the busy city street.

Regardless of the age or location of your house, don't miss any opportunity offered to learn about more than dates and deeds as you look back into its history. After all, appreciating the character and quality of a place involves more than molding profiles and paint scrapings.

7.

ORAL
HISTORY

In previous chapters, we discussed ways you can learn about your house by studying it yourself and by visiting dusty archives. Another approach is to ask around, pursuing a bit of local lore from those who are streetwise and historically curious—or who have simply lived nearby for many years.

What the elderly lady across the street tells you may well be colored a bit by her fondness for or dislike of previous denizens of your house or by the imperfections of the human memory. Even so, there probably is valuable information to be had. She may know when the kitchen was modernized or the outhouse burned down. She may have wonderful stories of eccentric uncles or batty aunts. They may be of no use to you in your renovation, but for many of us, a diverting anecdote is every bit as satisfying as a date or name from the distant past.

FINDING THE SOURCES

Tapping into private resources for the history of your house involves two steps: one, you have to find those resources, and, two, you have to use them effectively.

You may start with the previous owners and work back, although if the house is more than a hundred years old, you may wish to start earlier. Deeds and title searches (as described in Chapter 6) are your best source for names.

Often the best method for finding people familiar with the earlier life of your house is, simply, to ask around the neighborhood. Even if the population has changed radically, chances are there is at least one long-term resident. He or she may have valuable recollections, or may be able to provide you with names and addresses of other, long-ago residents.

In one instance I know of in Brooklyn Heights, in Brooklyn, New York, neighbors in a traditionally Irish neighborhood have provided virtually all the information necessary for a top-to-bottom reconstruction of a Victorian row house. It had been gutted in the 1960s, so little original interior detail was left. But through the kindness of elderly neighbors who provided recollections and the opportunity to inspect their own less renovated homes, a clear direction was developed for the reconstruction.

You read about the great flood, did you? Photographs like this one (of an upstate New York flood at the turn of the century) bring your imaginings to life.

Some of the sources cited in Chapter 6 may be useful here as well. Frequently local historical societies are peopled with senior citizens who care about their towns and neighborhoods because they've spent their lives there. But don't limit your local activity to the historical society.

Let it be known that you, the new folks in the old Smith house, are interested in the history of the place. You may meet both doddering old ladies and red-faced men who always seem to have had too much to drink; you may be surprised to be addressed by a stranger at the post office one day; and the information you get will vary from useful and accurate to utter hogwash. But it's worth a try.

THE INTERVIEW

Once you have determined who your sources are, you need to make contact to get the information you need. The approach is tricky, but the actual interview may be even more so. It's the most important step in the process; a poorly conducted interview is little better than none at all.

Do It on Site: If possible, conduct your interview at the house you are investigating. The house, its contents, or even the setting may elicit recollections that surprise both you and the interviewee. If infirmity or geography make that impossible, bring a site plan, photographs, documents, or even objects, such as heirlooms, with you. If you can't figure out what that little gewgaw or doohickey is, take it along and ask.

Use a Tape Recorder: Using a tape recorder may assure that you don't miss anything, but you must consult with your subjects first, as many people become suddenly tongue-tied when talking to tape recorders. Whether you use a tape recorder or take notes, be sure to amplify the record of the interview with your thoughts and conclusions on the same day the interview is conducted, either on paper or by talking into the tape recorder solo after the interview is completed.

Particularly when using a tape, valuable on-the-spot impressions can go unrecorded and be forgotten.

If you use a tape recorder, test it first. Turn it on, talk a minute or two, then run back the tape to make sure that it's working and that both your and your interviewee's voices can be heard clearly. Eliminate other noise sources like radios and television; shut the window to loud street noise.

Be Patient: This is especially true if you are an outsider who's just moved to town. For some people, an interesting and interested stranger is always welcome. For others, it takes time to trust a newcomer with secrets, even if they are not one's own.

If possible, make your contact through a mutual friend, preferably one who arranges and goes along on the first visit.

Let your interviewee set the pace. People have their own way of recounting events, their own mnemonic tricks for remembering. They also know what they want to tell and what is to be held in reserve.

Once you have the trust of your sources, you may learn a great deal. It may not all be germane to your house or to anything else you can think of, but you'll do well to think of it as deep background.

Begin with Someone Familiar: If possible, don't start with a crotchety stranger. Polish your questions and establish your confidence with someone with whom you feel comfortable.

Keep Track of Follow-ups: If your subject says, "You simply must talk with John Smith," make a note of it. Your goal is to learn as much as possible from the person you're interviewing and to develop new clues as you follow the trail.

Prepare Your Questions First: Make a list of the areas of inquiry that you wish to pursue in advance of your interview. If your interest is architectural, you'll want to note

167

down specific areas of the house to inquire about; if your concern is with genealogy, assemble those questions, too (see Key Questions, below).

Determine Common Ground: One variable you will encounter is the identification of houses by family. It's often useful shorthand to refer to "the old Smith place" rather than "the big house—it used to be yellow but now it's, ah,

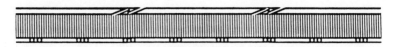

KEY
QUESTIONS

Who: Who do you remember living here? Do you recall hearing others talk about earlier residents? What were their names? What did they do? Where did they go? How many children did they have? Were they monied or impoverished? Were they house-proud or did they have a who-cares approach to their house?

Where: Do you remember when the addition(s) was (were) added? And why? Who did the work? Do you remember familiar tradesmen or names on panel trucks? What about other, similar houses next door or nearby?

Major Events: What would you say were the key events in the life of this house or the family in it? Fires? Marriages? Deaths? Wars? Bankruptcies? Crimes?

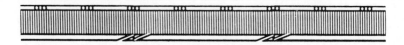

tan, I think—on the corner of that old dirt track I can never remember the name of." The Smith place it is, then . . . until you discover that another of your sources calls the same house the Jones mansion. Often it's a matter of generation: to someone who came to town long after the Smiths died, it is, quite logically, the Jones mansion. Be sure that the names you use not only for your house but any others that are mentioned identify them to your interviewees.

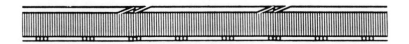

Modern Times: Do you remember the house *before* its remodeling(s)? When did they get rid of the wood stoves?

The Life of the House: Were animals kept nearby? Were there barns, sheds, a privy, or other outbuildings?

Exterior Finish: Do you remember when the house changed colors? When new siding was added? When a new roof was put on or chimney repaired? Was there a porch?

The Interior: Do you recall significant modifications indoors? New plaster, wallpaper, floor surfaces? When was the kitchen modernized? Was the furniture Victorian? What happened to it? Was there an auction?

Other Sources: Do you know anyone with whom I might talk who knew this house well in the past? Any sources of photos?

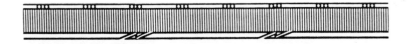

The Questions: You want to get your subject talking and comfortable and expansive, so at the beginning, avoid questions to which there are yes and no answers. Ask more specific questions later, and don't be concerned if the subject occasionally wanders off the track. You may discover other avenues for research.

Ask about your subject's involvement with the house: his or her first and last recollections of it, scenes of happiness or sadness which featured the place as a setting. Ask about other inhabitants. Were there changes in response to historical events like the Depression or a war? Were there family events of especial note? We all have a little of the reporter in us, so follow your instincts.

Be considerate: Don't get so involved with your pursuit of information that you forget the basic courtesies. Make sure the people you talk to understand that you appreciate their help. They may also enjoy the process as, after all, you are complimenting them by expressing an interest (even if indirectly) in their past. Do pay them the courtesy of appreciating their time and trouble.

Establish a Ground Zero: Start with questions concerning matters about which you know something. It won't be a waste of time. Your interviewee might know more about the topic than you do, and you will have a basis for judging additional information. If there are evident embellishments, other portions of this subject's recollections should be taken in perspective.

Often the oral history that is gathered from interviews is a blend of truth, confused recollections, and folklore. The good news is that extraordinary stories are told (my favorite is the one about the secret cellar in a barn in Middlefield, Massachusetts, in which a pair of insane twins are said to have been locked away for their entire adult lives). The bad news is that it isn't always possible to separate fact from fancy (did those twins really exist?).

No matter how much you come to enjoy the company of and trust the memories of your sources, be wary of believing everything they say. The human memory is a most fallible instrument, especially when many years have passed between the events in question and the present. The information might well have been second- or third-hand when your source got hold of it.

And another thing: know when to stop talking. Even if you truly love the sound of your own voice, you may be very disappointed if you listen to your tape and discover you didn't give your subject a proper chance to talk.

8.

AGE
INTO ACTION

By now, you probably know a good deal more about the age, character, or structure of your house than you did back on page one. Chances are that you have also realized how much has been changed (more than a little, and probably a lot). And you may have begun to think about restoring some of the bits that are gone and to consider how to preserve what is left.

Perhaps you also have a personal agenda to follow. Maybe you feel your family requires another bath or that the kitchen doesn't suit your needs. If the working systems are out-of-date, you may be considering a new heating system or electrical or plumbing work. Often it is simply a matter of taste: you know in your heart of hearts that to be happy in the house, changes just *have* to be made.

If you are like most people learning about old houses, you are also beginning to hear voices. Not ghosts of denizens past (not necessarily, anyway), but a disembodied chorus calling out to your conscience. The voices warn you of some sort of obligation to history, an obligation that goes unmentioned down at the houseware shop when they sell you reproduction light fixtures or replacement windows.

Those voices speak of historical courtesy. Though more

and more people today have developed a sense of obligation to the past, it isn't new. One of the men behind the English Arts and Crafts movement in the mid-nineteenth century, William Morris, accomplished a great many things in his life, as an artisan, a poet, a philosopher, even a fantasy writer of some note. But among his more significant contributions was the founding of the Society for the Protection of Ancient Buildings. Some of his thoughts back then still speak eloquently to concerns we face today.

"It has been most truly said that these old buildings do not belong to us alone," Morris wrote. "That they have belonged to our predecessors and will belong to our descendants unless we play them false. They are in no sense our property, to do as we like with them. We are only trustees for those that come after."

Certainly Morris's voice is one of those we hear as we contemplate renovations and their attendant demolitions. Another may be that of John Curtis, whom we met in Chapter 1. In his more than twenty-five years at Old Sturbridge Village, a restoration village in Sturbridge, Massachusetts, he has seen a change in the way concerned people treat old houses.

It used to be a matter of expunging what was there before returning to the original. "The tendency," Curtis says, "was to inflict your own personal taste, but that was a *personal* perception. [Now] if you can conserve at the same time as you strip, the generations to come can use their own judgment."

That's why preservationists frown upon gutting an old building. In doing so, much of the useless baggage of recent generations gets sent off to the landfill—but unfortunately countless clues go along for the ride. Large and small, they leave unrecognized and unrecoverable. Any changes made to an older house, whether conducted under the guise of remodeling, renovation, restoration, rehabilitation, or whatever, involves a certain amount of tossing out the proverbial baby-with-the-bath-water, so unnecessary demolition is to be avoided.

Another way to look at the problem is to consider a key criterion that many museum restorations and, increasingly, historically conscious homeowners require of any change. The notion is termed "reversibility"; every change made in an historic structure has to be "reversible." That word tumbles frequently from the lips of preservationists these days. As John Curtis puts it, "There is a new, broadly accepted awareness of the responsibility of the owner of an historic building to conserve the original." He isn't talking only about buildings in museum villages. An example of what he means is that if you are stripping off all the wallpaper, it probably makes sense to save samples of what is removed, at least of the earliest layers. You might consider leaving a section right on the wall, sealed beneath your new wall surface. It's a sort of time capsule for future historians.

An increasing number of areas throughout the United States have been designated "historic districts." The meaning varies, depending upon local statutes, but some such districts come complete with rigid standards for color selection and requirements for the submission of plans before any additions or renovations are initiated.

Unless you live in such a district, chances are you can do just about anything you want to your house short of violating building or fire codes. However, if your house is of a certain age, then the words of Messrs. Morris and Curtis should weigh somewhat heavily.

SOME ISSUES, SOME ANSWERS

This book doesn't pretend to tell you how best to take advantage of the age and character of your house; it's intended to help you recognize what's there rather than instruct you how to use what you find. But if you feel a desire to converse fairly with history and to respect the integrity of your home, the following basic concerns might help you as you consider making changes.

The Big Picture: Whether you are preserving, restoring, or remodeling, getting to know your house's secrets should be the first step in the process. Don't develop your plans until you know what you have. Do your research first, exploring documentary, stylistic, and physical evidence. Don't be satisfied with only one source of information, and make sure that the various sources corroborate one another. If you feel that your research is inconclusive, you may want to hire an expert consultant to study your house and property for you and make recommendations.

A full-fledged "historic structures report" prepared by an experienced preservationist is expensive. It involves many measured drawings and room-by-room inventories. For the remarkable historic building, it is advisable, but for a bungalow or vernacular Queen Anne, the appraisal needn't be so elaborate or expensive.

Remember, however, you can pay twice for bad renovations: once, when the contractor's bills arrive, and a second time, when you try to sell the house only to discover that a wrong-headed renovation has lessened the value of the place. So know thy house first, before embarking upon your changes.

Period Sources: Earlier in this book, passing mention was made of a variety of period source books. Many are still in print: books by the brothers Adam, Asher Benjamin, Andrew Jackson Downing, Gustav Stickley, and Frank Lloyd Wright are available in facsimile editions. Many books about these and other designers and builders are also available, as are such period sources as magazines and newspapers, especially for the Victorian age and after. (See For Further Research, page 189.) When you know how old your house is, it makes sense to know something about its era, too, so do some further homework. You'll find you have a better basis from which to make many decisions, whether it's about wallpaper or floor coverings or even room shape and ceiling height. Even if your goal isn't a precise restoration, having a sense of historical context can only help.

Qualified Professionals: Whether you are still at the research and study stage or you are about to restore, preserve, or renovate, hire an expert. Not just any contractor or architect will do: very few of them, despite claims to the contrary, really have a thorough knowledge of older houses. You want someone who does quality work *and* someone with first-hand experience in restoring vintage houses. Ask for references, and go and see the completed work. It's the only way to be sure.

What Is *That*?: This isn't a book about the law, but any volume about old houses has to be, at moments, about the crimes and misdemeanors that are oft committed on older structures. Some are obvious: destroying quality workmanship just for the sake of remodeling is one example. Others are less clear. You may regret it later if you commit as seemingly innocent an act as throwing away an unidentified piece of wood or iron. That lost object just might be a key clue, and its loss may prevent you from solving a puzzle and experiencing the rare pleasure of saying to yourself (and perhaps many others), "So *that*'s what it was."

Preservation Versus Restoration Versus Renovation: Decide exactly what it is you are going to do: Is it restoration, preservation, or renovation? These are important distinctions, although you are most likely to be doing some combination of preserving the old that remains, renovating to suit your needs, and, perhaps, restoring some of the old that is gone. But it is important that you make conscious and conscientious decisions.

Demolition: For many reasons, some of which we mentioned earlier, gutting for the sake of gutting is a bad idea. Who knows what evidence will be lost (to you and future owners of the house)? So try to save old plaster and work within the confines of what is there. On the other hand, when it comes to inappropriate later layers, don't hesitate to get rid of asphalt or aluminum siding, rotting decks, second-rate Colonial Revival doors on an earlier house, and so on.

Whatever demolition you do, however, make sure you don't miss any clues. Often old wood parts are reused in renovations, and they can indicate molding profiles or paint schemes. Look for the old beneath the more recent, and don't inadvertently throw out the good with the bad. If you don't know which is which, get some advice.

Original Work: Save quality workmanship. Unless it is in hopeless condition (and it rarely is, no matter how paint-coated and run-down the look), most old doors, plaster, hardware, floors, moldings, paneling, and other work are worth saving. And before you decree the stuff hopeless, get a second opinion. Quite surprising resurrections have been performed thousands of times, and often at a cost less than that of purchasing a new reproduction of the old piece(s).

Window replacement is a case in point. Today the wholesale substitution of new windows is commonplace. Often, the deed is done in the name of energy efficiency, but the result is usually a negligible saving in fuel costs, despite the claims of television advertisements. In many cases it does irremediable harm to an historic structure.

Windows are basic to the appearance of a house, in particular from the exterior. Replacing divided light windows (6/6s or even 2/2s) with single-sheet sashes transforms the elevation of a house. The appeal of the imperfect old wavy glass disappears. Equally important, the original geometry is lost as the proportions of the visible shapes change. Removing multiple-light sashes is rather like taking an eraser to some of the shading and intricate lines in an artist's drawing: none of us would advocate doing that to the details of, say, a Dürer woodcut, but the situations are similar.

If the windows have already been replaced, consider restoring them to their original configuration. If the windows are original but badly deteriorated, explore the possibility of having them restored. The cost may not be as great as you think, especially if you can remove the sashes from the frames yourself (generally not a difficult task). If the windows are drafty, perhaps weather-stripping alone will solve the problem. Storm windows are another option.

Original Intention: It isn't always possible to know or even guess at what the designers or builders had in mind. On the other hand, there are times when people callously contravene the original intention.

One example that comes immediately to mind is interior brickwork. Prior to this century, brick was rarely left exposed in the interior of houses except in the vicinity of a fireplace. In recent decades, the surfaces of brick walls have been liberated from their coatings of plaster or paneling and revealed for all to see. In apartment buildings, brick was commonly used in party walls that divided one building from the next. It is most often these brick surfaces, along with chimney breasts, that are exposed.

Therein lies an historical irony. As time makes the era of the handmade more and more remote, the handmade seems to exercise a greater appeal. In the days of the handmade, the desire was for ever finer surfaces, for regularity and polish. Those early craftsmen aimed to achieve hard and smooth finishes that to us are commonplace, but were to them impossible. Today we are proud to reveal what the masons of centuries past would have been embarrassed to have the public see.

In some cases, the brick-and-mortar surfaces found within walls are neatly coursed, with regular joints and well shaped bricks. More often, a lesser grade of material was used and less energy invested in making the finished product presentable. It was, after all, intended to be obscured beneath another surface. As a result, such long-hidden brick, when revealed, may or may not prove appealing.

Whether to expose or not is a matter of personal judgment. If the work is good, and the surface offers an appealing contrast to another in the room, perhaps it's a good decision. But in general, an old house is better served by regarding its builders' original intentions than by contravening them.

Mixing Periods: There's no law that says a mixture of time periods is gauche or "wrong." In fact, many of the most distinguished houses have "evolved" and today testify to the good design and the quality workmanship of several different periods.

No doubt your investigation will produce more than one date: the chronology of changes that were made to and the events that unfolded within your house offers a fourth dimension for you to factor into any renovation plans you have. The first date may be the most important, but there could be several of equal significance.

While it is just plain good sense to maintain a healthy respect for the old and for what is "period" to your house, don't let one era or style dictate all your decisions. You don't want to forgo all modern conveniences, as you would have to do in an eighteenth- or early nineteenth-century house: limited or no bathroom facilities, no electricity, no central heat, and so on. The old is not, by definition, good or even "right"; the new isn't necessarily inappropriate.

The initial construction may be the best, but often a later renovation by a wealthier resident introduces the best workmanship in a house. There is a considerable body of professional opinion among preservationists that later changes have a validity equal to the original. In any case, consider all the changes on an equal basis, then decide what works and what doesn't.

OBJECT LESSONS

Let's consider a trio of object lessons offered by three sets of homeowners who, step-by-step, made renovation decisions about their older homes.

Stephen Vanze and Judith Halsey live in Chevy Chase, Maryland. Both are architects who spend their days designing commercial spaces, but it's at home, in the simple bungalow they share with their two young children, that they have exercised their talents for domestic design.

Their 1911 house is a combination. It has the characteristic porch and posts of the bungalow but the hip roof of a Prairie School house. They began their remodeling in the rectangular combination-living-and-dining room that stretches from the front of the house toward the rear. They wanted to separate the room into two areas but not make it feel smaller, since the space is the most gracious in the house.

They chose to echo the porch, and built a columned screen of two columns and a pair of pilasters to bisect the room. It provides the illusion of a room division yet allows the eye (and all-important light) to move freely from the living room back to the dining area. Vanze found the columns at an architectural salvage shop. The price was reasonable and the columns date from roughly the same time as the house. Halsey's watercolors adorn the walls. The result is a space that is workable, appropriate to the style of the house, yet uniquely theirs.

For their kitchen renovation, the couple again looked to period sources for inspiration. They drew upon Craftsman style homes (many of which were, of course, bungalows) as well as the work of Frank Lloyd Wright. Their researches led them to select kitchen cabinets with glass doors of multiple lights. Lighting fixtures, too, were selected with regard to what Wright and others were designing and using in that era. The new roofline of the kitchen addition at the rear of the house also has the hip shape of the other volumes of the house. Many such touches and the use of appropriate materials, including wood floors, plaster walls, and simple wood moldings with profiles like those found in the home, give the extensively remodeled house a feeling of being very much of a piece and of a time without being dated.

Unlike Stephen and Judith, Judy and Jerry Grant aren't sure exactly how old their house is. They think it dates from about 1840, but some portions of the house may well be earlier. It's a simple two-story farmhouse, and when they moved into it in 1986, the building showed the effects of having been lived in (and remodeled by) numerous generations of people in New Lebanon, New York.

The Grants devised two different approaches to the upstairs and downstairs spaces. They found the original house had been changed very little on the second floor, and, as a result, they decided to leave it much as it was, except for the addition of a bathroom. The surprising surplus of closets in the master bedroom (a total of four) allowed them to do so without adding partitions or rearranging the nicely proportioned rooms.

The changes have been greater downstairs. The original chimney was gone, so they added a new one. The hearthstones were salvaged from a nearby house that had been demolished. Grant reused them, giving the firebox an appropriately time-worn stone texture. They found it was necessary to remove deteriorated floor members and to replace the floor in the living room, and in doing so, Grant used wide boards of various widths to mimic what had been removed. He even opted for using local pine and face-nailing with cut nails so the appropriate (rectangular) shape of the head would be visible on the surface of the floor. He painstakingly replicated the original architrave, chair rail, and baseboard moldings with hand planes.

The finished product is stunning. It doesn't pretend to be a precise restoration, yet the spirit of the old is there together with the clean lines of the new.

Don Carpentier and his wife, Denise, have recently moved into a New England Cape Cod style house that dates from 1789. The center chimney was gone when the Carpentiers bought the shell, but they reconstructed it, complete with bake oven and kitchen fireplace in the hall to the left and a second fireplace for the parlor to the right of the entrance. Upstairs are two small bedrooms. When the Carpentiers found the place, it was full of original details—paneling and doors and floors—so they felt no desire to remodel the existing space. Yet the place was simply too small. An addition was necessary.

For the Carpentiers, the decision was difficult. They didn't want to detract in any way from the little gem of a house, but something had to be done. They decided on a kitchen ell to extend from the center of the rear, its roofline running perpendicular to the main house. That way, the picture-perfect lines of the front elevation remain unchanged. On the exterior, they carefully matched materials. The ell roof, pitched steeply to conform with that on the original building, was made of matching cedar shingles, the walls faced with identical clapboard siding (all 4 to 6 feet in length). The 12/12 windows on the ell match those on the original house.

Inside the addition, the Carpentiers mixed the old with the not-so-old. The kitchen features a delicately carved Adamesque mantelpiece from about 1810, a likely date for a kitchen ell like theirs to have been added. While much of the architectural detail is of the same period, it was decided that the accoutrements of modernity did not have to meet the same standard.

"I didn't want to be silly by putting in electrified sconces," Carpentier said, adding that he wanted to avoid making the place feel "phony Colonial." His solution was to reach back to the days when electricity and modern appliances first began to dominate the country kitchen. He found a monitor-topped refrigerator and a long-legged, thirties gas stove. He and his wife managed to discover a great variety of the earliest possible "modern" electrical and other conveniences. The result is a house that looks very much as if one family had lived there for its nearly two hundred years, remodeling only when necessary.

My fifth-grade teacher went to great pains to explain to our class that it was impossible to "love" an inanimate object. Love was a two-way street, she told us, and *things* simply can't return one's affection.

I've always been inclined to agree with her, even in the face of assertions to the contrary in dictionaries, not to mention day-to-day usage. But after talking to all the people I've met in the last several years researching this book, I'm beginning to change my mind. Believe me, these people really love their houses.

They have invested incalculable time, energy, and (perhaps) love in gaining intimate knowledge of their homes. It is that familiarity, that sense both of what is and what was that is the major accomplishment of anyone who finds himself or herself involved in the care and feeding of an old house.

In pursuing their hobby, many house fanciers discover that history doesn't have to be intimidating. It doesn't consist solely of presidents and kings, but is made by little people, too, some of whom built and lived in their houses. History involves wallpaper and wavy glass and rusty nails—all of which deserve preservation, along with presidential documents and kingly crowns.

John Curtis is a man whose life's work is museum-quality restoration. But he also has his very own house on which to practice. Perhaps we can learn a little something from his patience.

"I live in an eighteenth-century house," he told me when I visited him and Old Sturbridge Village in the winter of 1988. I asked him how long he had owned it. "For twenty-two years," he replied.

I asked him if he had restored it himself, and he assured me he'd made moldings and hand-planed boards. He even told me a scary tale about a seeming heart attack he had one day when stripping paint. (He later concluded, after talking to some veteran painters, that what he'd experienced was "painter's colic.")

I also asked him how long he had taken to finish the house. "I'm not finished yet," he said, not the least bit sheepish.

That's another thing about old-house fanciers: the more they learn, the more they discover is left to do. Now, that's love, no matter what my fifth-grade teacher said.

GLOSSARY

architrave: In Classical architecture, the lowest portion of the entablature that sets immediately upon the columns or pilasters (originally, the architrave was the structural beam spanning the distance from column to column). Also, an ornamental molding covering the joints between the frame of a window or door opening and the surrounding wall surface. (See also **cornice** and **frieze.**)

balloon frame: A type of wood-frame construction in which the weight-bearing vertical members (the studs) extend from the sill at the foundation to the top plate. Common during the nineteenth century, it has been largely replaced since 1900 by the Western platform frame. (See drawing, page 14.)

bargeboard: The fascia board affixed to the verge of a roof to hide the structural carpentry. Also called the vergeboard, this board took on particular decorative significance in the 1840s and after in the Gothic Revival and other styles that used **gingerbread.** (See drawing, page 94.)

batten door: A door made of rows of vertical planks that were nailed or pegged to horizontal planks.

bay: The unit of space between a pair of cross frames (bents) in a timber-frame structure. (See also **bent** and drawing of timber-frame house, page 17.)

bead: A round, convex molding, often found on paneling and doorway and window trim in handmade houses.

beam: The main horizontal structural member in the construction of a frame house.

bent: In a timber-frame structure, one of the self-supporting units consisting of at least two legs (posts) and horizontal beams. Bents usually are at right angles to the length of the building, and divide the building into bays.

board-and-batten: A method of siding in which vertical boards are nailed to the frame of a house and narrow boards (called "battens") are applied over the joints between the boards. Board-and-batten siding is common in Gothic Revival frame houses.

boards: Milled wood cut to a thickness of 1 inch or less. (See also **dimension lumber** and **timber.**)

chair rail: The interior molding located at waist height that protects wall surfaces. (See drawing of molding locations, page 56.) Called a dado in Great Britain.

chamfer: An approximately 45-degree bevel put on a previously square-cut corner of a beam or other member.

clapboard: Siding material of horizontal wooden strips, often beveled and applied with the thicker edge overlapping the clapboard below.

clerestory windows: Window openings located in a row immediately above the top of the first story.

conveyance: The transfer of legal title by a deed, lien, mortgage, or assignment.

corner board: A vertical board at the corner of a house.

cornice: In Classical architecture, the topmost horizontal band of the entablature that projects at the crown of a wall. On a building's interior, the cornice is the molding located at the junction of the roof and wall surfaces. (See also **architrave** and **frieze.**)

course: A horizontal row of bricks, shingles, stones, or other building material.

deed: The signed legal document that conveys or transfers ownership of land.

dentil: One of a row of small blocks projecting from a cornice.

dimension lumber: Milled wood of a thickness more than 1 inch but not more than 4 inches. (See also **boards** and **timber.**)

double-hung window: A window in which the two sashes slide up and down within the plane of the wall. Prior to 1850, the upper sash was usually fixed; after that date, many double-hung windows had a system of counterweights hidden in the frame, allowing easy movement of both sashes.

double-pile plan: A house plan in which the building is two rooms deep. (See drawing, page 75.)

drywall: A prefabricated board of plaster sandwiched between layers of paper. Made in large (often 4 feet by 8 feet) sheets, it is attached to walls with nails or screws. Also known as gypsum board and by the trade name Sheetrock.

elevation: An architectural drawing indicating how completed interior or exterior walls will look; the point of view is that of an observer looking from a horizontal vantage.

ell: An extension to a building at right angles to the main section.

entablature: In Classical architecture, the assemblage of the horizontal bands of the cornice, frieze, and architrave, the elements immediately above (and supported by) the columns and capitals.

entasis: The slight swell of the shaft of a column.

escutcheon: The metal faceplate surrounding a keyhole, light switch, door knob, pipe, etc.

fabric: The physical material of a building; the implication is of the interweaving between the various component materials.

fanlight: A semicircular or half-elliptical window sash, often located over a doorway.

fenestration: The arrangement and proportioning of the openings (windows and doors) in a building.

finial: A decorative detail at the uppermost point of a pinnacle or gable.

frame house: A house in which the structural parts are wood or depend upon a wood frame for support.

frieze: The horizontal band between the cornice and the architrave in the entablature in Classical architecture.

gable: The end wall of a building formed by the eave line of a double-sloped roof.

gable roof: A roof with two roofing planes, joined at the ridge, that pitch evenly to opposite sides of the building. (See drawings of roof profiles, page 28.)

gambrel roof: A variation on the gable roof: the plane on each side of the ridge is broken roughly halfway down, and the lower half falls steeply to the eave. (See drawings of roof profiles, page 28.) While it was first found in America in New England in about 1650, the gambrel roof was probably most popular in the early years of the twentieth century in the Dutch Colonial Revival house. (See page 141.)

gingerbread: Decorative elements of intricately turned or sawn wood applied to the exterior trim. Especially popular during the Victorian era.

girt: In the timber-frame house, the girt is the horizontal beam that intersects the vertical posts at the second-floor level and that carries the second-floor joists. (See drawing of timber-frame house, page 17.)

grantee/grantor: In old deed terminology, the seller is the grantor, the purchaser the grantee.

half-timbered: A medieval building style identified by its exterior walls, which consist of an exposed frame of horizontal and vertical timbers with an in-fill of masonry, stucco, or **wattle-and-daub.**

header: A brick laid with its end outward.

186

hip roof: A gable roof with the ends shortened to form triangular surfaces. (See drawings of roof profiles, page 28.)

jamb: The lining at the side or head of a window, door, or other opening.

joist: One of a series of horizontal beams in a frame house that supports the floor boards and/or ceiling surfaces.

lath: The wood, metal, or other material attached to the frame of the building that acts to support the plaster in wet-wall construction. (See also **drywall**.)

mansard roof: A roof with two distinct pitches on all sides, the lower slope being sharply steeper than the upper one. (See drawing of roof profiles, page 28.) The name comes from the seventeenth-century French architect François Mansard.

mantel: The frame around the fireplace, whether made of wood, brick, or stone.

masonry: Brick, concrete, stone, or other materials bonded together with mortar to form walls, piers, buttresses, or other masses.

molding: A strip of wood used for finish or decorative purposes with regular channels or projections which provides a transition from one surface or material to another (e.g., baseboard, cornice, and casing moldings).

mortise: A cavity cut into the side or end of one framing member that forms a joint with the tenon cut into the end of a second member. (See drawing of mortise-and-tenon joint, page xviii.)

mullion: The vertical divider between multiple window sashes. Often confused with the term **muntin.**

muntin: The small wooden pieces that provide the divisions between the individual pieces of glass in a window sash. (See also **mullion**.)

newel: The large posts at the top, bottom, or turns of a stairway.

palladian window: A three-part window consisting of a taller center window, usually with an arched top, flanked by two shorter windows. Named after the sixteenth-century architect Andrea Palladio, it is also known as a Venetian window.

paneling: A wall surface consisting of panels set within a framework of vertical ("stiles") and horizontal ("rails") boards.

pediment: A shallow, triangular area formed at the gable end of a roof by the two roof lines, echoing the temple end of a Classical structure. A pedimented headpiece is sometimes found over doors and windows.

picture window: In the nineteenth century, a window assembled of pieces of stained glass was often termed a "picture window." The large, single-paned expanses of glass we refer to today as picture windows were introduced after World War II.

pilaster: A half-column, often with a flattened shape, affixed to a wall and projecting only slightly from it.

plat map: A top-view map of an area indicating locations and boundaries of individual properties, usually for tax purposes. (See also **plot map**.)

plate: The horizontal member that caps a wall structure and supports the rafters in a frame house. (See drawing of timber-frame house, page 17.)

plot map: A top-view drawing that identifies the boundaries and other significant aspects of the land on which a structure is built, as well as of the outline of the structure itself; also called a **site plan.**

post: A vertical structural member in a house frame. (See drawing of timber-frame structure, page 17.)

preservation: According to the Standards of the Secretary of the Interior (under whose auspices exist the Historic American Buildings Survey, the National Park Service, and the Preservation Assistance Division), preservation is, "The act or process of applying measures to sustain the existing form, integrity, and material of a building or structure, and the existing form and vegetative cover of a site. It may include stabilization work, where necessary, as well as ongoing maintenance of the historic building materials." (See also **rehabilitation** and **restoration**.)

quoin: Large stone (or wood elements carved to resemble stone) at the corner of a building.

rafter: One of a series of inclined structural members that support the roof, running from the exterior wall to the ridgepole. (See drawing of timber-frame house, page 17.)

reconveyance: A written, legal record that a mortgage has been paid off.

rehabilitation: According to the Standards of the Secretary of the Interior, rehabilitation is, "The act or process of returning a property to a state of utility through repair or alteration which makes possible an efficient contemporary use while preserving those portions or features of the property which are significant to its historical, architectural, and cultural values." (See also **preservation** and **restoration.**)

restoration: According to the Standards of the Secretary of the Interior, restoration is, "The act or process of accurately recovering the form and details of a property and its setting as it appeared at a particular period of time by means of the removal of later work or by the replacement of missing earlier work." (See also **preservation** and **rehabilitation.**).

ridgepole or **ridgeboard:** The horizontal member at the peak of the roof to which the top ends of the rafters are attached.

sash: The single, light frame that holds the glass in a window unit.

sidelight: One of a pair of windows flanking a door.

siding: The finished surface of an exterior wall, commonly clapboard or shingles.

sill: The lowermost member of a frame house, the sill is the large-dimension wooden element that rests directly on the foundation.

single-pile plan: An early plan in which the house was but one room deep.

soffit: The underside of an overhanging cornice.

stretcher: A brick laid lengthwise.

stud: One of a series of vertical wooden (or metal) structural members used as supporting elements in walls or partitions.

style: An architectural manner of using certain materials or methods to conform to certain standards; for example, the Greek Revival style uses decorations and shapes derived from ancient Greek sources.

tenon: The tongue-shaped projection at the end of a framing member that fits into a mortise. (See drawing of mortise-and-tenon joint, page xviii.)

timber: Milled wood of a thickness greater than 4 inches. (See also **dimension lumber** and **boards.**)

timber-frame: A type of wood-frame construction in which the weight-bearing members are timbers (see also **balloon** and **Western platform frame**). The rule until the mid-nineteenth century, the timber frame has now been largely replaced by stick-framing methods. (See drawing, page 14.)

trabeated: From Latin *trabes,* for beam, a trabeated structure is one that consists of large vertical posts that support horizontal beams. Trabeated structures range from the temples of ancient Greece and Stonehenge to today's steel-and-glass skyscrapers and America's millions of wooden houses.

wattle-and-daub: A wall surface consisting of interlaced twigs plastered with clay; once common in Britain, but rare in the United States. (See also **half-timbered.**)

western platform frame: A framing method in which the lumber and fasteners used are identical to those of the balloon frame; the distinction is that in the Western platform frame each floor is built independently. Thus, the vertical wall members, the studs, terminate at the ceiling of each story and new ones begin on the next floor level. (See drawing, page 14.)

FOR FURTHER
RESEARCH

I f you wish to learn more about old houses in America, there is an ever increasing number of sources to which you can refer. There are thousands of house museums, organizations, and individuals to help you better understand old houses, whether you are a homeowner, restorer, or simply a tourist. New books and magazines are appearing with stunning frequency.

There are also national sources to be drawn upon for specific tasks or avenues of research. In the following pages you will find an annotated list of potential sources of information, guidance, and help.

BOOKS AND MAGAZINES

It is always preferable to rely on sources that date from the period in which you are interested, so many period publications are cited. Our ancestors may have had some ideas that seem wrong or peculiar, but if they acted on them in their own time, then those notions are in some sense "correct." Secondary sources cited are those that, for the most part, provide accurate looks at the past and how things were done there.

Period Sources: A number of publishers are actively reprinting books by carpenters, designers, and manufacturers of earlier eras. Dover Publications, Inc. (180 Varick Street, New York, N.Y. 10014) has the largest such list. Write for a catalogue, as relatively few Dover books will be available in your bookstore.

Among the books of architectural interest from Dover are *The American Builder's Companion* (1827) by Asher Benjamin; *Victorian Cottage Residences* (1842) and *The Architecture of Country Houses* (1850) by Andrew Jackson Downing; *A Home for All*, Orson S. Fowler's paean to his brainchild, the octagon house; and *Craftsman Homes* (1909) by Gustav Stickley. *The Four Books of Architecture* by Andrea Palladio is also in print from Dover (in Isaac Ware's edition of 1738), and it's a key reference for understanding the inspiration for eighteenth-century American Georgian homes.

A variety of catalogues from the Victorian age have been reprinted by Dover and others. Among them are *Bicknell's Victorian Buildings* (1878) from Dover, *Picturesque California Homes* (1884) by Samuel and Joseph C. Newsom (Los Angeles: Hennessey & Ingalls), and *American Victoriana* (New York: Van Nostrand Reinhold).

While these books probably won't offer you practical guidance for the restoration of your house, you will almost certainly gain insight into the thinking of the men who conceived certain styles and inspired builders to work in certain ways.

Secondary Sources: Many fine books have been written about the evolution of the American house from a more recent vantage. If your house is from the Colonial era, one book that is likely to teach you something about it, regardless of geography, is *Early American Architecture: From the First Colonial Settlements to the National Period* by Hugh Morrison (New York: Dover, 1952). Two useful books about English style homes are *Early Domestic Architecture of Connecticut* by J. Frederick

Kelly (New York: Dover, 1924) and *The Framed Houses of Massachusetts Bay: 1625–1725* by Abbot Lowell Cummings (Cambridge, Mass.: Harvard University Press, 1979).

The best book about the Greek style is Talbot Hamlin's *Greek Revival Architecture in America* (New York: Dover, 1944). The series of books by William H. Pierson, Jr., under the general title *American Buildings and Their Architects* provides a quite detailed look at architecture in America. Volume 2, *Technology and the Picturesque, the Corporate and the Early Gothic Styles,* is of special interest for homeowners whose houses were built in the mid-nineteenth century.

If you're interested in the evolution of American building techniques, there are two classic works to read. *American Building: The Historical Forces that Shaped It,* 2nd ed. (Boston: Houghton-Mifflin, 1966), by James Marston Fitch, the retired dean of the school of architecture at Columbia University, covers social and economic trends as well as the history of building technology and provides a quite entertaining overview. *American Building: Materials and Techniques from the First Colonial Settlements to the Present,* revised ed. (Chicago: University of Chicago Press, 1982), was written by Carl W. Condit; it's a bit shorter on atmosphere than Fitch's book but richer in technological aspects.

Style Guides: Numerous handbooks intended to help you identify the style of a building have been published in recent years: nearly a dozen are generally available. The most comprehensive is *A Field Guide to American Houses* by Virginia and Lee McAlester (New York: Alfred A. Knopf, 1984). In its five hundred-plus pages, you'll find more than a thousand photographs and drawings.

For a brief (and largely photographic) review of American styles, you might consult *What Style Is It?* by John S. Poppeliers, S. Allen Chambers, and Nancy B. Schwartz (Washington, D.C.: Preservation Press, 1983); though a useful overview, this book features mostly high-style examples, so it is of limited assistance in identifying vernacular buildings. *Identifying American Architecture* by John J.-G. Blumenson is also quite brief, but it is very usefully illustrated with photographs that are dotted with labels to help you distinguish the ashlar quoins from the acanthus cornice (Nashville: American Association for State and Local History, 1981).

Publications: *The Old House Journal* and the National Trust publication *Historic Preservation* are two useful magazines for old-house fanciers. *OHJ* tends to offer quite specific, prescriptive advice (which paints and tools to use, techniques for common restoration/preservation tasks, potential sources for materials, and so on); *Historic Preservation* emphasizes feature articles and tends to be a bit more descriptive of people and places. Both make consistently interesting reading.

Period publications can be helpful, too. Many municipal public libraries will have *House Beautiful* and other magazines from the Victorian age. If your house is from the twentieth century, browse through the newpapers and magazines of the era, and learn what consumers were being offered.

Dating: The literature on the dating of houses per se is limited, to say the least. Most of the books cited above touch, at least tangentially, on the subject, but there is only one volume I know of devoted to dating in its entirety, a brief pamphlet titled *The Dating of Old Houses* (New Hope, Pa.: Bucks County Historical Society, 1976). Written in 1923 by a remarkable eccentric named Dr. Henry C. Mercer, the book is a reflection of his preoccupations with collecting and tools. It features photographs of nails and screws and hinges and plaster lath. While it errs a bit in making generalizations from the specific, Bucks County, Pennsylvania, to the general, the United States, it is a fascinating and seminal study.

ORGANIZATIONS

Many local historical societies have their own houses. Some are grand houses, others little more than abandoned buildings that have been filled with objects of no interest to anyone beyond those who live within the limits of the town itself. But invest the dollar or two donation, and go and look at every old house you can. Don't take everything you see as correct or period—you'll find incongruities and bad workmanship at even the best-intentioned and most expensive restorations. But seeing and experiencing old houses is invaluable.

There are also large-scale restorations across the country. Among them are Virginia's Colonial Williamsburg, Greenfield Village (see below), the Farmers' Museum in Cooperstown, New York, Old Sturbridge in Sturbridge, Massachusetts, and innumerable other restored/reconstructed collections of historic buildings. Even New York City has its own old-time village, Richmondtown Restoration on Staten Island, with its unparalleled collection of Dutch buildings. Visit these and other such places and learn from the buildings, collections, and interpreters.

Other organizations are active in other ways in educating the public about old houses. Among them are the following:

American Association for State and Local History, 172 Second Avenue North, Suite 102, Nashville, Tenn. 37204. The AASLH is an organization intended to serve those who work for historical societies and museums, archives, libraries, collegiate history departments, corporations, and other organizations concerned with preservation and historical matters. Dues vary from $25 to $100 a year, depending upon whether you are a student, senior citizen, professional, or a member of the general public.

In addition to running regional workshops, the AASLH is also an active publisher, issuing books; a bimonthly magazine, *History News;* a newsletter, *History News Dispatch:* technical leaflets; and reports of interest to both professional and lay audiences. Write for a catalogue.

Center for Historic Houses, 1785 Massachusetts Avenue, NW, Washington, D.C. 20036. A division of the National Trust (see below), the Center for Historic Houses aims to address the interests and concerns of the private owner of older or historic houses through informational services and educational programs. The Center conducts workshops and offers insurance for owners of fine historic residences. The Center does not maintain a separate membership, but all members of the National Trust may make use of its services.

Eastfield Village, Box 145 R.D., East Nassau, N.Y. 12062. Unlike Williamsburg and the other restoration villages, Eastfield is not open to the public. It is a study collection of more than twenty buildings and thousands of architectural and other artifacts of life in the Northeast in the pre-industrial era (the buildings date from 1789 to 1840).

Eastfield's reason-to-be is the workshops given there each summer. For fees that range from about one hundred to four hundred dollars, one- to five-day courses are given in restoration carpentry, architectural woodcarving, tinsmithing, grain-painting, plastering, and other early American trades and restoration skills. Write for a brochure.

Historic Deerfield, Box 321, Deerfield, Mass. 01342. Historic Deerfield was founded in 1952 "to promote the cause of education in and appreciation of the rich heritage of the early colonies." While the foundation was established in this century, the town itself was settled in the seventeenth century.

Today, Historic Deerfield has a dozen buildings open to the public; half are restored houses, half are exhibition buildings containing textiles and silver, furniture and clocks, and other collections of early American objects.

As well as a restoration at which one might spend many hours looking and learning, Deerfield is also a membership organization that offers forums and workshops (a recent one was titled, "What's in Grandma's Trunk? Textiles from the 19th and 20th Centuries"). There is a reference library, and the professional staff will offer advice regarding period furniture, decorative arts, architecture, and conservation/restoration procedures, if time permits.

Greenfield Village, Oakwood Avenue, P.O. Box 1970, Dearborn, Mich. 48121. Established by Henry Ford, Greenfield Village (and the adjacent Henry Ford Museum) occupy eighty indoor and outdoor acres. It's an immense collection of buildings and artifacts that collectively suggest something of the range of American ingenuity.

The village contains a range of structures, from a nineteenth-century tavern and farm to mills and forges and even the homes and workplaces of famous people (among them Noah Webster, Thomas Edison, and the Wright Brothers). The restoration is strongest on nineteenth-century America; there is also an extensive library and archive at the Henry Ford Museum. Write for a brochure.

National Building Museum, Pension Building, Judiciary Square, NW, Washington, D.C. 20001. Created by Congress in 1980, the National Building Museum was mandated to commemorate and encourage the American building arts, and it is funded by the federal government and by individuals (it costs students $15 to join, while a regular membership is $25). The museum puts on exhibitions, both touring and at its base in the Pension Museum (the giant, 1880s edifice constructed to handle the dispensation of benefits to Civil War veterans and survivors). It also publishes a newsletter, *Blueprints,* about activities at the museum and about building arts and preservation activities across the country.

National Park Service, P.O. Box 27127, Washington, D.C. 20013. The National Park Service, through its Preservation Assistance Division issues technical publications (for example, *Roofing for Historic Buildings,* 8 pages, 15 illustrations, $1 per copy). Write for a list.

National Preservation Institute, Inc., c/o National Building Museum. A nonprofit organization, the National Preservation Institute was founded in 1980, "to provide educational opportunities to complement higher education programs in historic preservation." It offers courses on historic buildings and districts, cultural landscapes, archaeology, and the history and practice of preservation. Courses are given at the National Building Museum in Washington, D.C.

National Register of Historic Places, National Park Service, U.S. Department of the Interior, P.O. Box 37127, Washington, D.C. 20240. Created under the 1966 National Historic Preservation Act, the National Register is the official list of the nation's districts, sites, buildings, and objects that are significant in American history, architecture, archaeology, engineering, and culture. A candidate for the National Register is nominated, then documented and evaluated according to the Secretary of the Interior's National Register criteria. When listed in the Register, the landmark is eligible for various kinds of federal help, ranging from grants for preservation and tax benefits to protection from surface coal mining.

National Trust for Historic Preservation, 1785 Massachusetts Avenue, NW, Washington, D.C. 20036. The National Trust is a private, nonprofit organization chartered by Congress in the National Historic Preservation Act of 1966. It is funded by several federal agencies, including the National Park Service and the U.S. Department of the Interior, as well as by membership dues ($15 annually), contributions, and endowment funds.

The organization is an advocate for preservation issues. It offers technical and financial advice to local historical societies, and lobbies Congress. It also protects numerous properties across the country, many of which are open as museums. It publishes the magazines *Historic Preservation* and *Preservation News* and administers the Preservation Press, which in turn publishes books concerned with architectural preservation.

Society for the Preservation of Long Island Antiquities, 93 North Country Road, Setauket, N.Y. 11733. The SPLIA maintains seven historic houses that are open to the public. It issues a newsletter and other publications; membership fees range from $5 for students to $25 for a family.

For an hourly, portal-to-portal charge, the SPLIA offers Long Island residents consulting services in paint analysis, historic architectural reviews, and dendrochronology.

Society for the Preservation of New England Antiquities, 141 Cambridge Street, Boston, Mass. 02114. It was founded in 1910 by William Sumner Appleton, a man described as "the nation's first full-time preservationist." He helped save a number of old buildings of architectural and historic merit, and today this preservation organization has twenty-four house museums open to the public and nearly two dozen "study properties."

The SPNEA is a membership organization which offers a number of services to the public, including education programs for school children, archival and visual materials, and a superb collection of New England decorative arts. It also publishes books and other materials, for both its membership and the general public. Membership is $15 for a student, $25 for an individual, $35 for a family.

The SPNEA has an Antiquities Conservation Center (185 Lyman Street, Waltham, Mass. 02154) that offers New Englanders a variety of services, including paint analyses, architectural reviews, and stenciling and plaster restoration. Write for a brochure.

Given limitations of space, the above is little more than a sampling of the available publications and kinds of organizations that exist. You're on your own from here: use your telephone book, regularly visit your local bookstore and library and hardware store, get tied into the network of old-house fanciers in your town or neighborhood.

In particular, make an effort to discover any sources of information about houses peculiar to your region. Even the national styles had many local variations, and chances are you are not the first one to be interested in a house like yours. Learn as much as you can about what others have done. You may avoid making restoration/preservation decisions you'll regret later.

INDEX

The words in boldface are defined in the glossary on page 185. Page references in boldface indicate the page number of an illustration or its caption.

196